MICRO OBEDIENCE, MACRO IMPACT

How Small Acts of Obedience Unlock Massive Kingdom Outcomes

by
Darrel Frater

The Center for Faith & Business Publishing
Tulsa, Oklahoma

Micro Obedience, Macro Impact: How Small Acts of Obedience Unlock Massive Kingdom Outcomes

Published by The Center for Faith & Business Publishing
Tulsa, Oklahoma
http://www.buildwithfaith.org/

ISBN: 979-8-89954-003-5
First Edition

Cover Design by Focus On Words, Inc.
Interior Design by Focus On words, Inc.
Printed in the United States of America

Dedication

To my incredible wife, Roselly.
You are a true embodiment of a Proverbs 31 woman.
Your strength, grace, and devotion to the Lord
shine in everything you do.

You inspire me to lead, to serve, and to stay faithful
to the call to the world and to our family.

None of this would be possible without
your obedience to follow Jesus.

Thank you for believing in me.

Table of Contents

Foreword

By Dr. Rodney Sampson

In the tapestry of innovation and faith, sometimes the smallest threads of obedience can weave the most transformational patterns. The title of this book, *Micro Obedience, Macro Impact,* perfectly captures a truth I've witnessed throughout my journey: when we honor God in the *micro*—in those everyday decisions to do right, to trust, to persevere—He multiplies it into *macro* results that can transform lives and even communities. In a world hungry for solutions to injustice and inequality, it often starts with a humble "yes" to a higher calling. Darrel Frater understands this deeply, and his story is a testament to how faith and business can intersect to create lasting impact.

I first met Darrel in 2020, when he was an entrepreneur in one of Opportunity Hub's founder programs during the pandemic. As the co-founder of OHUB, I have had the privilege of working with many driven entrepreneurs, but even among them, Darrel stood out. He radiated a passion for bridging faith and business—even then, you could tell his entrepreneurship was about more than profit. Our initial meeting quickly grew into a mentorship as Darrel pursued his venture capital journey. I watched him navigate challenges and opportunities with an integrity beyond his years, always guided by principle. Later, I recruited him to serve as a Venture Capitalist in Residence at OHUB, bringing his expertise and heart for service into our ecosystem. Throughout these years, I've been continually impressed by Darrel's commitment to *purposeful obedience* in every endeavor. He sought not just to build a company or a career, but to answer a calling.

Darrel is a man of visionary faith with a Kingdom mindset. By "Kingdom," I mean he carries a vision aligned with God's higher purposes – justice, love, and uplift for others. He understands that building a business isn't just about personal success; it's about *purpose.* In every conversation, his focus on economic justice comes through. He speaks about closing the racial wealth gap with the conviction of someone who knows this work is part of a divine mandate. Darrel sees entrepreneurship and venture capital as instruments to advance equity and opportunity for those historically left out. That alignment between his faith and his business mission is what gives him such credibility and power. He isn't merely talking about change; he's facilitating it – funding diverse founders, mentoring young entrepreneurs, and helping create pathways to generational wealth in marginalized communities. His vision is as principled as it is bold: to see a world where wealth and opportunity flow equitably, and to achieve this as an act of love and obedience to the calling God has placed on his life.

One of the qualities I admire most about Darrel is his unwavering integrity. In the high-stakes world of startups and venture capital, it can be tempting to cut corners or compromise values. Darrel never has. Time and again, I've seen him choose the harder right over the easier wrong. Whether it was honoring a commitment, being transparent in his dealings, or prioritizing impact over quick returns, he made decisions as if he was accountable to a higher authority – because he truly believes he is. This kind of integrity is rare, and it's foundational to the *macro impact* he's able to have. It reminds me of the scripture Luke 16:10, that teaches us if we are faithful with the small things, we'll be entrusted with greater things. Darrel's life exemplifies this principle. By being faithful and obedient in "small" matters, he has been given influence over much more. His increasing platform and success are not accidents of chance, but the byproduct of faithful stewardship and relentless obedience to God's guidance.

Crucially, obedience in Darrel's journey does not mean complacency or stagnation – it fuels *innovation*. He has always been willing to do something new, to step out of the comfort zone, when led by conviction. As an entrepreneur turned venture investor, Darrel pioneered creative approaches to funding and mentoring that defy the status quo. He listens for God's direction in the boardroom just as much as in the prayer closet. That blend of spiritual sensitivity and entrepreneurial grit produces innovation that serves a higher purpose. I've seen him back startups that others overlooked, because he could envision their potential to solve real problems and create wealth for the underserved. In doing so, he demonstrates that obeying a God-given vision often means being an *agent of innovation* in the marketplace. This is faith in action: not a passive waiting, but an active building of new solutions, new companies, and new paradigms – all while anchored to unchanging principles.

Darrel's commitment to generational wealth is another aspect of his Kingdom vision. He doesn't just talk about lifting individuals; he talks about lifting *generations.* He and I both know from our work that wealth in our communities has to be intentionally cultivated and passed down. It brings to mind Proverbs' wisdom that a good person leaves an inheritance for their children's children. In practical terms, that means creating businesses, funds, and opportunities that outlast us – that benefit not only our own families but also our broader community for centuries to come. Darrel is actively engaged in that work. Whether through his family office or the ventures he supports, he is helping lay a foundation of wealth and knowledge that future generations of black and brown entrepreneurs and investors can build upon. This isn't just economic strategy; it's spiritual legacy. It's about honoring the sacrifices of those who came before us and obeying the call to uplift those who come after us. In Darrel, I see a leader who understands that true success is measured by the **impact** and **inheritance** we leave behind, not just the accolades we collect for ourselves.

In *Micro Obedience, Macro Impact,* Darrel Frater has poured the wisdom of his journey onto these pages. He challenges the conventional definitions of success and dares to redefine success as *surrender*—a complete surrender to the Lord's will in our careers and enterprises. In a culture that often glorifies hustle for hustle's sake, Darrel issues a clarion call to instead align our hustle with Heaven's purposes. He shows that when you align your purpose with your faith, you unlock a power to create change that mere ambition alone could never achieve. This book is a bold invitation to faith-driven entrepreneurs and leaders everywhere: to fuse your business pursuits with biblical principles, to let every investment and innovation be guided by a sense of higher mission. Darrel's stories and insights show how walking in obedience – even in the smallest steps – positions you for divine multiplication. Reading this foreword is just the beginning; as you delve into the chapters ahead, you'll find practical strategies, heartfelt testimonies, and inspiring examples of what happens when one dares to put God first in business.

As someone who has devoted much of my life to the intersection of faith, entrepreneurship, and inclusive innovation, I am profoundly encouraged by Darrel's contribution here. His voice is a fresh wind in our ongoing pursuit of economic justice. He speaks with the authority of experience – not only as a man of faith, but as a proven founder and investor who has *done the work*. The principles he shares aren't theoretical for him; I've seen him live them. That authenticity is what makes this foreword easy to write and this book important to read. Darrel's alignment with the mission to close the racial wealth gap isn't just professional – it's personal, spiritual, and palpable in every page of his book. He is, in every sense, a *principled disruptor*: using the tools of finance and technology to serve the cause of equity, and doing it all with an eye towards eternity.

It is my honor to introduce and endorse *Micro Obedience, Macro Impact*. In these pages, you will not only get to know Darrel's heart and vision, you will also be equipped and inspired to amplify your own. My hope is that as you read this book, you allow its message to stir you to action. Let it remind you that no act of obedience is truly "micro" when it's directed by God – each one is a seed that can yield a harvest beyond what you imagine. The path to closing wealth gaps, to righting injustices, to building thriving enterprises that bless communities, is paved by those willing to say "yes" to the still, small voice calling them forward. Darrel Frater said "yes," and it has led him to a life of significant impact.

May you be galvanized by the wisdom in this book to say "yes" in your own journey. Say yes to innovation that aligns with your values. Say yes to leadership that puts people over profit. Say yes to the kind of purposeful, faith-fueled obedience that Darrel champions – the kind that will ripple out and echo for generations. My friend and protégé, Darrel, has written something special here. I believe it will empower you to turn your **micro obedience** into **macro impact** for the glory of God and the good of others.

Dr. Rodney Sampson
Executive Chairman & CEO,
Opportunity Hub (OHUB)

Preface

I didn't set out to write a book...

What you're holding is the result of many small yeses—quiet moments of surrender that didn't always make sense at the time, but were absolutely necessary. Writing this wasn't about obligation. It's all about obedience.

Like many Kingdom-minded entrepreneurs, I've felt the tension between building something great and remaining deeply submitted to God. Between the pressure to achieve and the call to slow down and listen. Between what the world defines as success and what Heaven rewards as faithfulness.

This book was born from that tension.

Each page represents a lesson learned, a conviction tested, and a truth revealed through real-life faith and business experiences. Not as someone who's figured it all out, but as someone who's learning to build with God rather than ahead of Him.

My prayer is that this book meets you right where you are—in your boardroom, your kitchen table, your quiet time, or your next big decision. And that as you read, you'd hear God's invitation to partner with Him in deeper, more obedient ways.

This is a book about building—but more than that, it's about trusting.

About following God in the small things, so He can do big things through you.

Let's not be afraid to build differently.

—Darrel Frater

Introduction

We live in a culture that celebrates big moves—scaling fast, breaking records, and going viral. But in the Kingdom, it's often the smallest acts of obedience that delights God the most.

That's the heartbeat of this book.

Not grand gestures. Not flashy success.

Just quiet yeses that change everything.

I didn't write this book because I had all the answers. I wrote it because I kept hearing God whisper, "Do this. Do that. Speak to them." And every time I did—even when it didn't make sense—He revealed something bigger than I could have planned on my own.

As a faith-driven entrepreneur, I've wrestled with the pressure to perform, the temptation to compare, and the urge to build faster than God was moving. But time and again, I've learned that obedience is the most powerful business strategy you'll ever apply.

Micro Obedience, Macro Impact is a devotional roadmap for Kingdom-minded leaders. Each chapter explores a biblical principle, a real-life business application, and an invitation to obey in the small things. Because when you obey God at His word—no matter how insignificant it feels—He honors it with supernatural outcomes.

This isn't just a leadership book.

It's a discipleship journey.

It's for the builder who prays before pitching.

For the entrepreneur who wants an eternal return on investment.

For the believer who doesn't just want to be successful—they want to be surrendered.

So whether you're at a crossroads, scaling something new, or starting again—this book is for you. Read it slowly. Reflect often. Obey boldly.

And watch what God does through your yes.

—Darrel Frater

OBEDIENCE OVER OUTCOMES
PROVERBS 3:5-6

1

Obedience Over Outcomes

Scripture Anchor: Proverbs 3:5-6

"Trust in the Lord with all your heart and
lean not on your own understanding;
in all your ways acknowledge Him,
and He will direct your paths."

In the fast-paced world of business and entrepreneurship, outcomes are everything. Metrics, milestones, and KPIs dominate our decisions. We're trained to think in results—profit margins, return on investment, and growth trajectories. But in the Kingdom of God, the equation is different. God is not merely interested in what we produce—He's deeply concerned with how we obey.

This chapter is about learning to choose obedience over outcome. It's a countercultural approach, especially in spaces where success is typically defined by visible results. But Scripture flips the narrative: our job is obedience, and God handles the outcome.

Micro Moments, Eternal Impact

Have you ever had a gut feeling—just a small prompting—that you later realized changed everything? Maybe it was reaching out to someone unexpectedly, holding back a harsh response, or taking a job that made no sense logically. These are the moments I call *micro obedience*—those small, Spirit-led actions that don't make headlines but move heaven.

I remember when I was wrestling with a career decision that made absolutely no sense on paper. The opportunity seemed too small. The salary was a fraction of what I had envisioned. But in prayer, God whispered, "Trust Me." I chose obedience—not because I understood the outcome, but because I trusted the One directing my path. That decision became a domino in a chain reaction of divine opportunities.

Micro obedience often feels insignificant. But when aligned with God's timing, it positions us for macro impact. The simple act of saying "yes" to God when no one is watching opens doors that no man can shut. That's what makes obedience so powerful—it invites divine collaboration into our natural circumstances.

When we study Scripture, we see this pattern consistently. Moses' obedience to return to Egypt led to Israel's freedom. David's faithfulness as a shepherd positioned him for kingship. Esther's bold step before the king saved a nation. Each of these pivotal moments began with obedience that seemed small or even illogical in the moment. God has always used small acts of obedience to accomplish mighty things.

Deep Dive: Noah – Obedience Before the First Drop

Let's take a closer look at a story that perfectly illustrates this theme: Noah and the ark.

In Genesis 6, God tells Noah to build an ark because a flood is coming. Up until this moment, there had never been rain of the magnitude God was describing—some scholars even argue it had never rained at all. Yet Noah obeyed. He spent decades constructing a massive boat with no rain in sight, under public scrutiny, surrounded by skeptics.

Noah didn't know how or when the flood would come. He didn't have the full blueprint of the outcome. All he had was a word from God. That's the essence of obedience—acting on divine instruction without full understanding.

Imagine the discipline, faith, and mental endurance it took to obey every single day. The building of the ark was a long, repetitive, and often thankless task. But Noah's obedience had generational consequences. His act preserved humanity. It fulfilled God's plan. It demonstrated trust.

Genesis 6:22 says, *"Noah did everything just as God commanded him."* This simple verse contains the formula for divine success. Noah didn't partially obey. He didn't delay. He didn't negotiate terms. He obeyed fully and immediately.

In your business, God may be asking you to build something that doesn't make sense yet. He may be prompting you to prepare for a season that hasn't arrived. And like Noah, you may face ridicule, doubt, or uncertainty. But obedience precedes breakthrough. Noah's reward didn't come at the beginning—it came when the rain fell and the ark was ready.

And here's the most profound part: the rain came not *because* Noah obeyed, but *after* he obeyed. The obedience didn't bring the rain—it prepared him for it. That's the power of trusting God with the process.

Obedience When It Doesn't Add Up

Proverbs 3:5-6 challenges us to lean *not* on our own understanding. Why? Because understanding is limited. We only see what's right in front of us; God sees the full picture. When we obey based on understanding, we cap our potential to what *we* can comprehend. But when we obey God—even when it doesn't make sense—we tap into supernatural alignment.

Business research even reflects this principle. Companies like Chick-fil-A have made bold decisions, like closing every Sunday, that defy conventional logic. Yet their obedience to values has created a culture of rest, loyalty, and record-breaking profitability. They chose purpose over pressure, and God honored it.

Other business leaders like Alan Barnhart have modeled this too. After studying what the Bible says about wealth, Barnhart decided to cap his income and donate half of his company's profits to God's work. That small act of obedience—a financial ceiling—became the foundation of a business that grew at 25% annually for over 20 years. His story proves that obedience often unlocks favor, even when it doesn't follow conventional wisdom.

Obedience that doesn't add up on paper is often the one that adds up in eternity. In a world of logic, God calls us to trust. In a world of data, He invites us to discernment. When you respond to divine instruction over your own intelligence, you release outcomes that only God could engineer.

Obedience Breaks the Idol of Control

For many of us—especially entrepreneurs—control is an idol. We like predictable outcomes and calculated risks. But obedience requires surrender. It forces us to admit that *we are not in charge*. In my own journey, I realized that I had turned my intellect into an idol. If a plan didn't make sense to me, I dismissed it. But that mindset limited what God could do through me.

Choosing obedience means saying, "God, I trust You more than I trust my own strategy." That's not reckless—it's faithful. It's not lazy—it's dependent. And it's the only way to experience the kind of success that heaven endorses.

When you relinquish control, you give God space to operate. Control says, "I need to know what's next." Obedience says, "God knows what's next." One is exhausting; the other is freeing. And in business, peace is a competitive advantage. Obedient leaders lead with calm confidence, not fear-based urgency.

Think about Abraham. He was told to leave his homeland and go "to a place I will show you." There was no map. No concrete plan. Just a command to go and a promise to bless. That's the essence of obedience. You go before you know. You trust before you see. And that trust breaks the grip of fear, anxiety, and self-reliance.

God Measures Success Differently

Luke 16:10 tells us that faithfulness in small things qualifies us for more. That means God sees obedience—especially the small, hidden kind—as success. While the world chases the big win, God honors the small yes.

In the venture capital world, we often look for traction—users, revenue, market demand. But what if God's measure of traction isn't numbers, but faithfulness? What if your biggest spiritual return on investment isn't your valuation but your obedience?

When we obey in micro ways—returning a phone call, preparing diligently for a meeting, acting with integrity when no one's watching—we build the character that God can trust with more. And often, it's these unseen acts that become the platform for visible influence.

We want influence before we build integrity, but God sees things differently. He's not just developing your business—He's developing you.

In God's economy, trustworthiness is the currency of promotion. Are you faithful with the little—your current role, your limited resources, your small audience? If so, God will entrust you with more. He doesn't look for talent first. He looks for trust.

Trust Is the Foundation

Trust is the currency of obedience. If you don't trust God, you won't obey Him—at least not consistently. That's why Proverbs 3:5-6 is so powerful. It's not a call to reckless action; it's a call to anchored trust. When we trust Him with *all* our hearts, we surrender our need for full understanding and step into divine alignment.

This doesn't mean you discard wisdom. God gave you a mind for a reason. But trust means that when your wisdom collides with God's instruction, you choose Him every time.

Every major shift in my life came from a moment of micro obedience. Not one of them made total sense in the moment. But over time, the pattern became clear: trust plus obedience equals destiny. And that formula holds true in any boardroom, startup, or calling.

This trust must be cultivated. Spend time in prayer. Stay rooted in the Word. Surround yourself with godly counsel. When your relationship with God is strong, obedience becomes a reflex, not a wrestle.

Questions for Reflection

1. Where is God asking me to take a step of obedience, even if I don't understand the full picture?
2. Have I made an idol out of understanding or control?
3. How can I cultivate a lifestyle of trusting God's guidance in my daily work?
4. Am I being faithful with the small responsibilities in front of me today?

Activation: Obedience Inventory

Take 15 minutes today to list 3 areas in your business or personal life where you've been hesitant to obey God. Pray over each one and ask for the faith to take the next small step.

Then, take one step—no matter how small—toward obedience in each area this week. Journal the results. Often, clarity follows obedience, not the other way around.

Final Thoughts

The outcomes you want are often waiting on the obedience you've been resisting. God doesn't need your strategy—He needs your surrender. And as you obey, even in the smallest things, you invite heaven to back your efforts.

Obedience doesn't always guarantee immediate results, but it always guarantees alignment with God's will. And that alignment opens doors no strategy can.

In a world obsessed with outcomes, dare to value obedience. Dare to believe that a small yes to God can shake nations. That a quiet act of faithfulness can write the next chapter of your legacy.

So choose obedience—even when it doesn't add up. Because with God, every micro obedience leads to macro impact.

Closing Prayer

Father, thank You for reminding me that success in Your Kingdom starts with obedience. I confess the times I've chased outcomes more than Your voice, and leaned on my own understanding instead of trusting in You. Help me to surrender control, release my need for certainty, and walk by faith—even when I can't see the full picture.

Make my heart sensitive to Your leading. Teach me to trust You with the details I don't understand. Give me courage to take steps of obedience, no matter how small they may seem. Let my life, my work, and my leadership be a reflection of trust in You. And may every micro act of obedience I offer bring glory to Your name and impact far beyond what I can measure.

In Jesus' name, Amen.

A FIRM FOUNDATION
MATTHEW 6:33

2

A Firm Foundation

Scripture Anchor: Matthew 6:33

"But seek first the kingdom of God and His righteousness, and all these things shall be added to you."

In a world that prioritizes hustle, ambition, and the pursuit of success, the idea of putting God first can seem counter-intuitive. Yet this command from Jesus in Matthew 6:33 is not just a call to devotion—it's a strategy for provision. When we put God first, everything else falls into place. The challenge is learning to trust that promise.

This chapter is about building your life and business on Kingdom priorities. It's about what happens when your calendar, your money, your energy, and your decisions reflect a clear hierarchy: God first, then everything else. The result? A life of alignment, peace, and supernatural favor.

The False Security of Self-Priority

We live in a culture that celebrates independence. "You've got to look out for number one." "Chase the bag." "Grind now, shine later." These are the mantras of our day. But Kingdom culture is different. In God's economy, we don't chase blessing—we follow obedience and let blessing chase us.

Jesus doesn't say "Don't seek anything." He says, "Seek first the Kingdom." Seeking first doesn't mean we ignore our goals or responsibilities. It means we anchor them in the right priority. When God is first, everything else finds its proper place.

When God is not first, everything feels out of order. We're constantly chasing, comparing, and striving. We may even achieve success—but without peace. And that's the difference. Success without peace is a counterfeit reward.

This isn't just a theological idea—it's a practical reality. Putting God first might mean making difficult decisions: turning down a lucrative opportunity that would compromise your values, or stepping away from a relationship or deal that is misaligned with your purpose. And yet, it's in these moments of surrender that you build a foundation that can sustain divine promotion.

Deep Dive: Elijah and the Widow at Zarephath

One of the most striking examples of this principle is found in 1 Kings 17. Elijah, the prophet of God, is told to go to Zarephath where he will be fed by a widow during a time of famine. When Elijah arrives, he meets the woman gathering sticks. He asks her for a drink and then boldly says, "And bring me a piece of bread."

Her response is heartbreaking: "As surely as the Lord your God lives, I don't have any bread—only a handful of flour in a jar and a little olive oil in a jug. I am gathering a few sticks to take home and make a meal for myself and my son, that we may eat it—and die."

Elijah responds with a Kingdom principle: "Don't be afraid. Go home and do as you have said. But first make a small loaf of bread for me... For this is what the Lord says: 'The jar of flour will not be used up and the jug of oil will not run dry until the day the Lord sends rain.'"

That moment is the Matthew 6:33 principle in action. *Seek God first, and the rest will be added.* Elijah, as God's representative, is asking the widow to give to God first—to feed the prophet before feeding herself or her son. And miraculously, her obedience leads to provision.

This story is a powerful illustration for business leaders and entrepreneurs. There will be seasons where it feels like you only have "a handful of flour." Resources are tight, risk is high, and fear is knocking. But in those moments, the choice to prioritize God—through generosity, Sabbath rest, ethical decisions, or Spirit-led strategy—invites supernatural provision.

Her obedience was not logical. It was radical. But that one act unlocked a promise that sustained her household for many days. In God's hands, scarcity becomes sufficiency. Our priority becomes the platform for our provision.

Rewriting Your Internal Order

Many people put God in the mix, but not first. We say He's Lord, but we function as if He's a consultant—someone we call on in emergencies or big decisions, but not in our daily routines.

What does it practically look like to seek God first?

- It means starting your day with Him, not your inbox.
- It means praying before you plan.
- It means surrendering opportunities before signing contracts.
- It means asking God what success looks like, rather than assuming it's just profit or prestige.

This heart posture creates clarity. When God is first, decisions become simpler. You're not swayed by every offer, trend, or temptation. You operate with a different kind of discernment because your compass is calibrated to God's will, not the world's approval.

This kind of obedience often requires sacrifice. But it's in those very sacrifices that God proves Himself faithful.

He provides, multiplies, and sustains in ways you could never orchestrate on your own.

Living the Priority Principle

Putting God first is not an emotional high. It's a daily discipline. It's less about what you say and more about what your life reflects. If someone examined your calendar, your bank statements, your thought life, and your relationships—would they see God as your first priority?

In business, this looks like beginning your week in prayer, inviting God into meetings, and refusing to compromise your values even under pressure. It means giving generously, even when it tightens margins. It's choosing rest over burnout, purpose over profit, and trust over hustle.

Alan Barnhart, who we discussed in Chapter 1, modeled this principle well. He and his wife made a commitment to cap their lifestyle and give away the rest—even as their business exploded in size and profitability. They didn't just acknowledge God with their lips—they prioritized Him in their decisions. And because of that, they watched "all these things" be added unto them.

It wasn't always easy, but their story shows us something important: when you give God your best, He ensures you lack nothing. He stretches what you surrender and blesses what you build with Him at the center.

Practical Ways to Put God First in Business

1. **Start the Day with God** – Begin each workday with prayer and Scripture. Invite God into your meetings, decisions, and goals.
2. **Tithe and Give Generously** – Return a portion of your income to God through your local church or causes He leads you to support. Giving is one of the most tangible ways to put God first financially.
3. **Honor the Sabbath** – Resist the pressure to always be "on." Set aside time to rest, reflect, and recharge with God at the center.
4. **Seek God in Decision-Making** – Before launching a new project, hiring a new team member, or making a big move, pause and ask: "God, what do You want me to do?"
5. **Serve with Integrity** – Let every client interaction, contract, and conversation reflect Kingdom character.
6. **Surround Yourself with Godly Counsel** – Wise mentors and peers who share your values help keep your priorities aligned.
7. **Measure Success God's Way** – Don't define progress solely by revenue or reach. Define it by obedience, peace, and purpose.

When You Put God First...

When you put God first, you stop operating out of anxiety and start operating out of trust. You begin to experience what Jesus promised in the second half of Matthew 6:33: "...and all these things shall be added to you."

"All these things" include the needs you're stressing over—finances, opportunities, team growth, open doors, provision. God knows what you need. He's not withholding—He's waiting for your priorities to align with His.

And this isn't just about money. It's about wholeness. Peace. Purpose. Legacy. When you put God first, you don't just succeed—you thrive.

Some of the most successful Kingdom-minded entrepreneurs will tell you that they didn't chase what they received. They chased God—and He orchestrated the opportunities.

There's something magnetic about obedience. It attracts divine partnership. It aligns your natural efforts with supernatural outcomes.

Questions for Reflection

1. What does your current schedule say about your priorities?
2. Are there areas in your business or personal life where God has taken a back seat?
3. What would it look like for you to put God first in a difficult decision you're facing right now?
4. What fears keep you from prioritizing God fully?
5. Who can hold you accountable to keep God first in your life and leadership?

Activation: The First Fruits Challenge

This week, identify one area where you can intentionally give God your "first." Whether it's the first 30 minutes of your day, the first 10% of your revenue, or the first decision in a key project—start with God.

Write down the area you chose, what obedience looks like in that space, and track what changes over the next 7 days. Journal any shifts in your clarity, peace, or progress.

Then, commit to extending this habit beyond the challenge. Make first-fruits obedience a lifestyle, not a one-time experiment.

Final Thoughts

God doesn't want to be your business partner. He wants to be your CEO. The one calling the shots. Directing the strategy. Carrying the weight. And when you seek Him first, everything else follows.

You may not always see immediate results. But the promise is clear: *put God first, and everything you truly need will follow.*

That's the divine equation for favor—and it begins with a simple decision: God first. Just like the widow who obeyed Elijah, your act of obedience may seem costly, but it will never go unrewarded. In God's economy, what you give up for Him always returns multiplied.

So don't just make Him part of your life. Make Him the priority. When God is first, everything else finds its rightful place—and the overflow is greater than anything you could have built on your own.

Let your business, your budget, your brand, and your time all speak one truth: God is first here. And because He is, nothing will be lacking, and nothing will be wasted.

Closing Prayers

Father, thank You for the powerful reminder that when we seek You first, everything else falls into place. I confess the moments when I have allowed busyness, fear, or ambition to cloud my priorities. I want to be a person who puts You first in all things—in my thoughts, my schedule, my finances, and my leadership.

Teach me to trust You more deeply and obey You more quickly. Help me resist the temptation to chase success without Your direction. Give me the strength to make difficult decisions that honor You, even when the cost is high.

May my business and my life reflect the truth that You are not just a part of my plans—you are the center of them. Let every area I steward be built on the foundation of Your wisdom, timing, and presence. And may others see the fruit of a life fully surrendered to You.

In Jesus' name, Amen.

WORK AS WORSHIP
COLOSSSIANS 3:23

3

Work as Worship

Scripture Anchor: Colossians 3:23

> “Whatever you do, work at it with all your heart, as working for the Lord, not for human masters."

In today’s culture, work is often viewed as a means to an end—a way to earn money, gain recognition, or build influence. But in God’s Kingdom, work is more than a paycheck; it’s a platform for worship. Every meeting, every task, every email becomes sacred when we understand who we’re really working for.

Colossians 3:23 reshapes our mindset: "Whatever you do, work at it with all your heart, as working for the Lord, not for human masters." That one verse flips the script on how we approach the marketplace. When we work as unto the Lord, work becomes holy.

This chapter explores how to restore sacredness to your everyday grind, revealing how your job can become a daily act of devotion.

Work is God's Idea

Before sin ever entered the world, there was work. Genesis 2:15 says, "The Lord God took the man and put him in the Garden of Eden to work it and take care of it." That means work wasn't a punishment—it was part of paradise.

God designed work to be fulfilling, creative, and fruitful. He created us in His image to build, lead, and steward. Work is not the result of the fall—only toil is. In Christ, we have the opportunity to redeem the meaning of work and return to its original design: worship through stewardship.

When we understand that work was present in Eden, we stop seeing it as a necessary evil and begin to see it as a divine calling. The enemy has tried to distort the purpose of work by connecting it solely to survival, status, or stress. But God sees your daily labor—your spreadsheets, service calls, product designs, patient care, or parenting—as sacred ground.

Deep Dive: Joseph's Journey from Servant to Steward

If anyone had a reason to resent work, it was Joseph. Sold into slavery by his brothers and falsely accused by Potiphar's wife, Joseph found himself working in environments far beneath his gifting. But his story is a blueprint for Kingdom excellence.

In Genesis 39, we read that "the Lord was with Joseph, and he prospered." Even as a slave in Potiphar's house, Joseph worked with integrity and diligence. He didn't wait for a promotion to give God his best—he gave his best in the pit. His attitude wasn't dependent on his title; it was rooted in his trust in God.

When Joseph was promoted, it was because he had already proven trustworthy with little. And even in prison, he continued to serve with excellence. Eventually, God used his work ethic and wisdom to elevate him to second-in-command over all of Egypt.

Joseph's life teaches us that work done in obscurity is never wasted. When we serve faithfully in hidden seasons, God is positioning us for public influence. But more importantly, He's shaping our character to sustain it.

One of the most profound aspects of Joseph's story is his consistency. No matter where he was—Potiphar's house, prison, or the palace—his approach to work didn't change. He brought the same diligence to cleaning a house that he did to managing a kingdom. That's the heart of worship.

Worship Is More Than a Song

We often limit worship to music or Sunday gatherings. But biblically, worship means "worth-ship"—to attribute value and honor. When you give your best at work because God is worthy of it, that's worship. When you treat your coworkers with patience and grace, that's worship. When you build systems, solve problems, and serve customers with joy, you reflect the heart of a Creator who brings order out of chaos.

Romans 12:1 calls us to present our bodies as "a living sacrifice, holy and pleasing to God—this is your true and proper worship." That includes your hands, your mind, your skills, your business deals, your meetings, and your to-do lists.

God isn't waiting for you to clock out to be honored. He wants to be glorified in the way you clock in. Every day is an opportunity to worship with your work.

Why Excellence Matters

Excellence is not about being perfect—it's about doing your best with what you've been given. When we operate in excellence, we reflect a God who does all things well. Excellence is a witness. It speaks of your values. It sets you apart.

Daniel 6:3 says, "Now Daniel so distinguished himself among the administrators... by his exceptional qualities that the king planned to set him over the whole kingdom." Daniel's worship was visible in his work. And in a foreign land under pagan rule, his excellence gave him a platform to influence culture.

Your integrity in negotiations, your consistency in hard seasons, and your attitude in adversity all speak. They declare who you work for. And when God is your boss, the standard should be different.

Excellence doesn't mean overworking or burning out. It means maximizing what you've been given. The parable of the talents in Matthew 25 reveals that God rewards faithfulness and fruitfulness. The servant who invested what he was given heard, "Well done, good and faithful servant." That should be our goal—not applause from man, but affirmation from Heaven.

Reclaiming the Sacred in the Secular

Too often, we compartmentalize faith and work. But Jesus didn't die just for your Sunday morning—He died for your Monday too. If Jesus is Lord of your life, then He must be Lord of your labor.

We must reject the notion that our job is "just business." No, it's Kingdom business. Whether you're a CEO, a teacher, a developer, a driver, or a barista—your work matters to God.

This means:

- Showing up on time is spiritual.
- Meeting deadlines is worship.
- Treating clients with respect is Kingdom culture.
- Delegating well and leading with clarity honors God.

You don't need to quit your job to do ministry. Your work *is* your ministry. And your workplace is one of the greatest mission fields you'll ever enter.

When people see you handle stress with peace, correct mistakes with humility, and navigate decisions with wisdom, they see the Gospel in action. Your life becomes the sermon.

Practical Ways to Worship Through Work

1. **Consecrate Your Workday** – Begin with prayer. Invite the Holy Spirit into your agenda.
2. **Practice Excellence** – Go the extra mile, not for applause but for the glory of God.
3. **Honor Leadership** – Submit with respect and integrity, even when it's hard.
4. **Serve Others Well** – Make your customers, team, and clients feel seen and valued.
5. **Avoid Complaining** – Cultivate an atmosphere of gratitude and encouragement.
6. **Model Integrity** – Let your yes be yes, your no be no, and your handshake mean something.
7. **Rest Regularly** – Don't idolize hustle. Obey the rhythm of rest God established for your good.
8. **Mentor Someone at Work** – Use your influence to lift others up, not just yourself.
9. **Document God's Faithfulness** – Keep a journal of how God shows up in your daily work.
10. **Celebrate Small Wins** – Acknowledge progress and give God glory along the way.

Questions for Reflection

1. How do I currently view my work? Is it worship or just a job?
2. Where have I allowed mediocrity or apathy to take root?
3. What would shift if I approached my work as sacred every day?
4. How does my current work ethic reflect my faith?
5. In what ways can I honor God through my interactions with coworkers, clients, and leaders?
6. What "small" task can I start doing with greater intentionality today?
7. Who can I encourage, disciple, or support through my workplace?

Activation: Make Your Desk an Altar

This week, set aside time to pray over your workspace. Dedicate your office, cubicle, laptop, tools—whatever you use for work—to God. Say: "Lord, this belongs to You. Use me here for Your glory."

Write down one task you usually rush through or neglect, and commit to doing it with excellence this week as a form of worship.

Then take note of how your peace, productivity, or attitude shifts. Track what God does when you shift your posture.

Go one step further: Identify one coworker or client you can serve or bless this week. Ask God to show you what they need, and be willing to be the vessel He uses.

Final Thoughts

You don't need a pulpit to change the world. Your job is your platform. Your excellence is your sermon. Your work ethic is your worship.

God is not looking for part-time believers—He's looking for full-time worshipers. People who honor Him in the office, the boardroom, the warehouse, and the startup garage. People who bring the Kingdom to work.

Joseph didn't become a leader because of ambition. He became a leader because he treated every job—even slavery and prison—as sacred. When you work as unto the Lord, you become promotable in Heaven's economy.

So tomorrow morning, don't just get ready for another day at the office. Step onto holy ground. Because when you commit your work to God, He commits to working through you.

Closing Prayer

Lord, thank You for the reminder that my work is not just a task—it's an offering. Forgive me for the times I've separated my faith from my work, or treated my job as mundane. Today, I choose to see every assignment as holy and every interaction as a chance to reflect Your love.

Teach me to serve with excellence, integrity, and humility. Help me approach each day with a heart of worship and a desire to bring You glory. Let my discipline, diligence, and creativity point others to You.

Use my job, my business, and my gifts as instruments of Kingdom impact. May my work be a testimony to Your goodness and a tool to advance Your purposes. Remind me daily that when I work for You, no effort is wasted.

Empower me to model what it looks like to be a believer who doesn't just work hard but works holy. And may the culture around me be changed because I chose to worship You with my work.

In Jesus' name, Amen.

THE STEWARDSHIIP
STANDARD
LUKE 16:10

4

The Stewardship Standard

Scripture Anchor: Luke 16:10

> "Whoever can be trusted with very little can also be trusted with much, and whoever is dishonest with very little will also be dishonest with much."

In Kingdom business, stewardship is the foundation upon which responsibility, influence, and multiplication are built. God isn't just looking for gifted leaders—He's looking for faithful stewards. Those who handle what they have with excellence, integrity, and a long-term Kingdom perspective.

The world applauds ownership, but God celebrates stewardship. Ownership says, "This is mine to use."

Stewardship says, "This is God's, and I'm entrusted to manage it." That one shift in mindset changes everything—from how you run your business, to how you spend money, to how you treat people.

This chapter is about living up to the Stewardship Standard. It's about managing what's in your hand as if it belonged to Heaven—because it does.

What Is Stewardship?

Stewardship is the God-honoring practice of managing resources, responsibilities, and opportunities with excellence and purpose. It goes beyond financial management—it's about your time, your influence, your gifts, your relationships, and your business.

Psalm 24:1 reminds us, "The earth is the Lord's, and everything in it." That includes your company, your paycheck, your calendar, and your calling. You are not the owner—you are the manager. When you embrace this, every decision becomes spiritual. Every dollar you spend, every hire you make, every deal you close carries eternal weight.

God is less interested in how much you have and more concerned with how you handle what you've been given. Faithful stewardship creates a foundation for sustainable success, both spiritually and professionally.

Deep Dive: The Parable of the Talents

In Matthew 25:14–30, Jesus shares a story about a master who entrusts three servants with different amounts of wealth (talents) before going on a journey. One receives five talents, another two, and the last one talent—each according to their ability.

The first two servants invest their talents and double what was given to them. When the master returns, he commends them: "Well done, good and faithful servant! You have been faithful with a few things; I will put you in charge of many things."

But the third servant, out of fear, hides his talent in the ground. He doesn't lose it—but he also doesn't multiply it. His inaction is seen as unfaithfulness. The master rebukes him for being wicked and lazy and takes away the talent he was given.

The lesson? Stewardship is not about playing it safe—it's about faithful multiplication. God expects us to do something with what He's given us. Playing small isn't humble if it disobeys God's expectation.

Whether you're managing millions or mentoring one person, you are accountable for what you've been entrusted with.

And consider this: The master gave "each according to their ability." God doesn't compare you to someone else's stewardship—He evaluates you based on what He gave *you*. That should relieve pressure and inspire responsibility. Stewardship is never about volume; it's about faithfulness.

The Mindset of a Steward

A steward sees life through the lens of accountability and purpose:

- **Time is not just a schedule—it's a tool for Kingdom impact.**
- **Money is not just currency—it's a resource for ministry and mission.**
- **People are not just employees or clients—they're image bearers to be served and empowered.**

When you operate with this perspective, excellence becomes your default. Waste is no longer acceptable. Mediocrity is not an option. You recognize that everything you've been given is a test, a trust, and a tool for advancing God's Kingdom.

This mindset also redefines success. Instead of asking, "What can I get out of this?" the steward asks, "What does God want to do through this?"

And it compels you to steward *yourself* well—your health, your habits, your mental focus. Because you can't sustain Kingdom stewardship on an empty tank.

Faithful in the Small

Luke 16:10 isn't just a feel-good verse—it's a principle of promotion in God's Kingdom. If you're not managing your current level of responsibility well, why would God increase your influence?

Being faithful in the small means:

- Responding to texts and emails with integrity.
- Honoring financial commitments even when it's hard.
- Investing in the growth of one team member.
- Operating in excellence even when no one is watching.

God often tests us in private before trusting us in public. When no one else is clapping, God is still watching.

Remember, David was anointed king but continued to care for sheep until his appointed time. His faithfulness in obscurity prepared him for prominence. He didn't need a platform to practice stewardship—he used a pasture.

That's the beauty of God's process: what you do with a little reveals what you'd do with a lot.

Stewarding Finances with Purpose

Financial stewardship isn't just about budgeting—it's about aligning your money with your mission. Every dollar is a disciple. Every investment is a statement of trust.

- **Tithing and generosity** show that God is your source, not your bank account.
- **Wise budgeting and savings** reflect that you plan for the future but trust God for provision.

- **Giving sacrificially** stretches your faith and breaks the grip of materialism.

Money is a magnifier. It reveals what's already in your heart. That's why God tests us with money before He trusts us with ministry.

When you prioritize Kingdom principles over profit, God expands your reach. Your business becomes a conduit for impact—not just income.

Start by asking: "Does my budget reflect my values? Is my giving growing alongside my income? Have I sought God about how to steward surplus?"

In Luke 12:48, Jesus says, "From everyone who has been given much, much will be demanded." Prosperity comes with responsibility. The more God gives you, the more accountable you become to use it for His purposes.

Practical Ways to Live the Stewardship Standard

1. **Audit Your Resources** – Review how you're using your time, money, energy, and influence.
2. **Set Stewardship Goals** – Create measurable goals for generosity, delegation, or mentoring.
3. **Budget with a Kingdom Lens** – Allocate funds not just for growth, but for impact.
4. **Evaluate Your Systems** – Are your operations stewarding people's time and talents well?
5. **Mentor Future Stewards** – Multiply your mindset by raising up others with stewardship DNA.

6. **Establish Accountability** – Invite trusted voices to speak into how you manage what God has entrusted to you.
7. **Plan for Succession** – Stewardship includes legacy. Are you training others to carry the vision forward?
8. **Celebrate Progress** – Mark and honor the wins, even the small ones. Celebration is part of stewardship.

Questions for Reflection

1. Do I view myself as an owner or a steward of my business and resources?
2. How have I managed the "little" things God has entrusted to me?
3. Where have I been fearful to act, like the servant with one talent?
4. What systems or structures in my life or business need realignment with Kingdom stewardship?
5. Who in my life can help hold me accountable to steward well?
6. Is there an area I've overextended due to poor stewardship of time or energy?
7. What does stewardship look like for my family, team, or organization?

Activation: Stewardship Inventory

This week, conduct a "stewardship inventory." Choose three areas of your life—time, money, and relationships—and evaluate how you're managing them:

- Are they aligned with God's priorities?
- Are they being wasted, underutilized, or mismanaged?
- What is one practical change you can make in each area to steward it more faithfully?

Write it down, pray over it, and implement the first step within 48 hours. Invite a mentor or accountability partner into the process.

Bonus Challenge: Choose a resource (money, tool, platform, property) and ask God how He wants you to use it for someone else's benefit. Then obey.

Final Thoughts

God is not asking you to do more than He's given—but He is asking you to do your best with what He has. Stewardship isn't just a principle for growth—it's a pathway to Kingdom influence.

You don't have to have the most, but you do need to manage well what you do have. Because in the Kingdom, promotion comes to the faithful, not just the gifted.

Whether you're in a season of five talents or one, be found faithful. Because how you steward this season sets the stage for your next one.

The world promotes charisma, but God promotes character. And the character of a good steward is what makes a life—and a legacy—God can trust.

Closing Prayer

Father, thank You for entrusting me with resources, relationships, and responsibilities. I recognize that everything I have is a gift from You, and I want to steward it in a way that brings You glory.

Forgive me for the times I've wasted opportunities or held onto what You asked me to release. Teach me to be faithful with what's in my hands. Give me courage to multiply, not bury, the talents You've entrusted to me.

Help me to manage my business, my time, my finances, and my influence with excellence and integrity. May I never take ownership of what belongs to You. And when You return, may You find me faithful.

Empower me to think generationally, lead humbly, and build wisely. Let stewardship be my signature and legacy.

In Jesus' name, Amen.

DILIGENCE IN THE DETAILS
PROVERBS 13:4

5

Diligence in the Details

Scripture Anchor: Proverbs 13:4

> "The soul of the sluggard craves and gets nothing, while the soul of the diligent is richly supplied."

In a world of instant gratification and shortcuts, diligence is often overlooked. Yet in the Kingdom of God, diligence is not just a trait—it's a spiritual discipline. It's the engine behind fruitfulness, the steady hand that builds legacy, and the daily act of honoring God with focused effort.

This chapter is about reclaiming the power of diligence—not just as a pathway to success, but as a mark of faithful leadership. When we combine faith with follow-through, dreams become results, and promises become platforms for God's glory.

The Value of Diligence

Diligence is defined as careful and persistent effort. In Scripture, it's tied to abundance, wisdom, leadership, and divine favor. Diligence isn't just about working hard—it's about working with consistent excellence, even when no one is watching and the results are slow.

Proverbs 12:24 says, "The hand of the diligent will rule, while the slothful will be put to forced labor." In other words, diligence determines destiny. It separates those who lead from those who must be led. Not because of superiority, but because of stewardship.

God honors the diligent because diligence honors God. It's a reflection of His nature—He is a God who finishes what He starts.

Diligence also reflects discipline—the ability to do what is needed, even when motivation is absent. And discipline is a spiritual muscle we strengthen through repetition. You don't build diligence in a moment; you build it in the mundane.

Deep Dive: Nehemiah and the Rebuilding of the Wall

One of the most compelling biblical examples of diligence is Nehemiah. Upon hearing that the walls of Jerusalem were broken down, Nehemiah wept, fasted, and prayed.

But he didn't stop there. He received permission from the king, mobilized resources, and led the people in rebuilding what others had ignored.

Despite facing opposition, mockery, and threats, Nehemiah kept building. He posted guards, encouraged the workers, and refused to be distracted. In Nehemiah 6:3, when his enemies tried to lure him away from the project, he responded, "I am doing a great work and I cannot come down."

That's the voice of diligence. It's focused. It's anchored in purpose. It doesn't entertain distractions.

Remarkably, Nehemiah and his team completed the wall in just 52 days—a task many thought was impossible. Why? Because he partnered prayer with persistence. Vision with vigilance. Strategy with sweat.

Nehemiah didn't just have a calling—he had the diligence to carry it out.

And even after the wall was completed, Nehemiah continued leading the people with vision, reform, and worship. Diligence doesn't stop at the finish line—it sustains what has been built.

Diligence vs. Hustle

It's important to distinguish between diligence and hustle. Hustle is driven by fear, scarcity, and the need to prove something. Diligence, on the other hand, is grounded in faith, stewardship, and obedience.

Hustle says, "If I don't grind 24/7, I'll fall behind." Diligence says, "If I stay faithful to what God gave me, He'll multiply it in due season."

Hustle leads to burnout; diligence leads to fruit.

God never called us to hustle culture. He called us to a pace of grace—where diligence meets divine timing. That's where you experience true productivity: not just busy hands, but fruitful lives.

Diligence honors boundaries. It works hard *and* rests well. The diligent don't chase every opportunity—they steward the right ones. This is key for sustainable success.

Faith Requires Follow-Through

James 2:17 reminds us that "faith without works is dead." In business, this means you don't just pray over your idea—you put in the hours to build it. You show up consistently, improve your craft, and honor your commitments.

Too many visions die in the gap between inspiration and execution. Diligence is what closes that gap. It turns ideas into impact.

This means:

- Following up when others forget.
- Delivering excellence when you feel tired.
- Planning your week with intention, not waiting for motivation.
- Managing your time like it matters—because it does.

Faith will spark your journey, but diligence will sustain it.

Faith says, "God will do it." Diligence says, "Let's prepare for it." Both are required.

When Diligence Feels Discouraging

Every diligent person faces seasons where progress feels slow or invisible. You're planting seeds, but the harvest hasn't come. You're doing the right things, but the breakthrough hasn't shown up.

Galatians 6:9 offers encouragement: "Let us not grow weary in doing good, for in due season we will reap, if we do not give up."

That's the promise of diligence. *Due season* is coming—but only if you don't quit.

This is where many fall off. Not because they lacked talent, but because they lacked tenacity. Diligence requires spiritual endurance. It means trusting that every act of obedience, every hour of preparation, every email and meeting matters in the long-term picture.

Diligence is the decision to continue doing good when applause is absent and outcomes are uncertain.

Long-Term Thinking in Diligence

Diligence sees beyond today's to-do list. It has a vision for legacy. It asks, "What am I building that will last?"

This mindset challenges us to:

- Build systems, not just solutions.
- Document processes, not just projects.
- Train others, not just lead alone.
- Write down vision, so others can run with it (Habakkuk 2:2).

Long-term diligence prepares succession. If your diligence ends with you, your impact dies with you. But if it multiplies through others, your legacy lives on.

Practical Ways to Practice Diligence

1. **Plan Your Week with Purpose** – Start each week by reviewing priorities and scheduling focus blocks.
2. **Break Big Goals into Daily Actions** – Don't wait for big wins. Show up daily with intentionality.
3. **Track Progress, Not Perfection** – Measure your momentum, not your milestones.
4. **Use Time Blocks** – Allocate specific windows for email, deep work, and recovery.
5. **Pray Over Your Task List** – Commit your plans to God and ask Him to establish your steps (Proverbs 16:3).
6. **Guard Your Focus** – Eliminate distractions. Every "yes" requires a hundred "no's."
7. **Finish What You Start** – Be known as someone who delivers. It builds trust and honors God.
8. **Honor Rest** – True diligence includes recovery. Rest is resistance against burnout and pride.

9. **Create Daily Rituals** – Set a rhythm that builds consistency and reduces friction.
10. **Celebrate Small Wins** – Acknowledge progress. Celebration fuels continued effort.

Questions for Reflection

1. Where in my life or business have I grown passive or inconsistent?
2. Have I mistaken busyness for diligence?
3. What are the “walls” God has called me to rebuild, and how am I progressing?
4. How do I respond when progress is slow?
5. In what ways can I better guard my time and focus?
6. Who can help hold me accountable to diligent habits and standards?
7. What daily routine could increase my consistency and focus?

Activation: The Diligence Tracker

This week, choose one project or habit you’ve been neglecting. Commit to working on it for 30 minutes a day for 7 straight days.

- Track your consistency.
- Note how your mindset and momentum shift.
- Reflect on what God shows you during the process.

At the end of the week, evaluate: What fruit came from simply showing up daily?

Then, identify a system or routine that can help you continue that diligence going forward.

Bonus Challenge: Teach one person this principle of diligence. Discipling multiplies discipline.

Final Thoughts

Diligence isn't sexy—but it's supernatural. It's not always applauded—but it's always rewarded. God uses the diligent to build what lasts.

In a culture addicted to quick results, diligence reminds us that slow growth is still growth—and it's often the most sustainable. You may not see the full picture yet, but if you remain faithful, God will finish what He started in and through you.

Be like Nehemiah. Stay on the wall. Ignore the noise. Build anyway.

Because the world needs more than dreamers—it needs finishers. And in the Kingdom, finishers are forged in the furnace of diligence.

Closing Prayer

Father, thank You for calling me to a life of faithful diligence. Forgive me for the times I've allowed laziness, distraction, or discouragement to steal my momentum. Renew my commitment to work with excellence—not just for results, but as an offering to You.

Give me strength when I feel tired, focus when I feel distracted, and courage when I feel overwhelmed. Help me to honor You not only with my big ideas, but with my daily habits. Let my work ethic reflect Your faithfulness, and let the fruit of diligence bring glory to Your name.

I trust that in due season, You will honor every seed I've sown in faith. Until then, help me to keep showing up, keep building, and keep trusting.

In Jesus' name, Amen.

IMAGE BEARING
INTEGRITY
PROVERBS 10:9

6

Image Bearing Integrity

Scripture Anchor: Proverbs 10:9

"Whoever walks in integrity walks securely,
but whoever takes crooked paths will be found out."

In a world obsessed with personal branding, optics, and curated perfection, the call to live and lead with integrity is more countercultural than ever. But in the economy of God, character still counts. Integrity is the invisible infrastructure that holds your influence together.

This chapter explores why integrity is greater than image—because it's the one thing you take with you into every room, every season, and every opportunity. When your private world is aligned with your public life, God can entrust you with more than you ever imagined.

The Foundation of Integrity

Integrity means being whole, undivided, and consistent. It comes from the Latin word *integer*, which means complete or whole. A person with integrity isn't perfect, but they are the same on the inside as they are on the outside.

We live in a time where perception often overrides truth. Social media rewards the appearance of virtue more than the practice of it. But in God's Kingdom, authenticity matters more than applause.

Proverbs 11:3 says, "The integrity of the upright guides them, but the unfaithful are destroyed by their duplicity." Image can elevate you temporarily, but only integrity will sustain you long-term.

Walking in integrity means choosing consistency over convenience. It's a lifestyle, not a moment. It shows up when you return the shopping cart, when you're honest on your tax return, and when you speak well of someone who doesn't deserve it. Integrity isn't just a value—it's a discipline.

Deep Dive: Daniel's Unshakable Integrity

One of the greatest biblical examples of integrity is Daniel. A Jewish exile living under Babylonian rule, Daniel rose through the ranks of a foreign government without compromising his faith.

Daniel's story begins with a small decision: he resolved not to defile himself with the royal food and wine (Daniel 1:8). That act of quiet obedience became the foundation for a life of integrity. He remained faithful to his values even when it meant going against the culture.

Later, when political rivals tried to trap him, they found no fault—except in his devotion to God. They passed a law outlawing prayer, knowing Daniel would disobey it. And they were right. Daniel continued praying three times a day, just as he always had.

He didn't protest. He didn't hide. He didn't conform. He simply lived with integrity—and ended up in a lion's den.

But God delivered him. And the king who condemned him later declared the greatness of Daniel's God. That's what integrity does. It may cost you in the short term, but it will always protect you in the end.

Daniel didn't just have favor—he had faithfulness. And that faithfulness built trust with God and man. It preserved his influence and positioned him to lead.

The Fragility of Image

Image is about perception. It's what others think you are. Integrity is about truth. It's who you really are.

Image is fragile. It can be built in years and shattered in moments. Integrity is resilient. It strengthens under pressure.

We've seen it time and time again—leaders who fall not because of their lack of talent, but because of their lack of integrity. When your character can't support your platform, collapse is inevitable.

Don't build a business that requires you to pretend. Don't chase visibility at the expense of accountability. What you compromise to gain, you'll eventually lose.

Psalm 15 asks, "Lord, who may dwell in your sacred tent? Who may live on your holy mountain?" The answer? "The one whose walk is blameless, who does what is righteous, who speaks the truth from their heart."

God promotes those He can trust—not just those who are popular.

Integrity gives you staying power. It's what keeps your team loyal, your family proud, and your legacy strong. It's what allows you to show up in every room with peace, knowing you have nothing to hide.

Integrity in Business Decisions

Integrity shows up in how you:

- Pay your employees
- Report your taxes
- Handle confidential information
- Speak about your competitors
- Deliver on promises
- Handle your finances when no one is looking
- React under pressure

Cutting corners might boost short-term results, but it always damages long-term impact.

Ask yourself:

- Do my contracts reflect fairness?
- Do I honor my word, even when it's inconvenient?
- Do I correct mistakes, even when I could ignore them?
- Would I trust me if I were on the other side of the deal?

Integrity doesn't mean perfection—it means humility. When you fall short, you take ownership. When you're wrong, you make it right.

This kind of leadership earns trust, loyalty, and respect. It also opens doors that talent alone never could.

Internal Integrity: Private Obedience

The most important form of integrity is the kind no one sees. Jesus warned the Pharisees that they were like whitewashed tombs—clean on the outside but full of decay on the inside (Matthew 23:27).

In the marketplace, this looks like:

- Polished pitches but broken prayer lives
- Perfect websites but poor character
- Charisma without conviction

God isn't impressed by image. He's drawn to integrity.

Private obedience is the greatest indicator of public influence. Who you are when no one is watching determines how much God can trust you when everyone is watching.

Integrity means:

- Telling the truth even when it hurts
- Returning extra change at the register
- Saying no to unethical deals
- Refusing to exaggerate results
- Keeping your commitments even when they become inconvenient

It means doing what's right because it's right—not because it's rewarded.

Long-Term Rewards of Integrity

Proverbs 28:6 says, "Better the poor whose walk is blameless than the rich whose ways are perverse." In the Kingdom, the currency of character is greater than cash flow.

Here's what integrity produces:

- **Security** – You sleep well when you live right.
- **Stability** – People can count on you.
- **Credibility** – Your word carries weight.
- **Legacy** – Your life outlives your resume.
- **Favor** – God can promote you without apology.

The rewards of integrity often show up in seasons of testing. When others cut corners, you remain steady. When temptation calls, you say no. And in time, God rewards your faithfulness with favor.

Just like Daniel, your integrity will speak for you—even when you're not in the room. You don't need to chase platforms—God will call your name when the time is right.

Practical Ways to Build Integrity

1. **Invite Accountability** – Surround yourself with people who will challenge and correct you.
2. **Audit Your Motives** – Ask: "Why am I doing this? What's driving this decision?"
3. **Keep Your Word** – Say less. Do more. Honor every commitment.
4. **Practice Transparency** – Be honest about mistakes. Share challenges. Build trust.
5. **Honor Boundaries** – Respect people's time, money, and trust.
6. **Protect Confidentiality** – Keep private things private.
7. **Repent Quickly** – Don't cover up sin. Confess it and grow.
8. **Build in the Dark** – Do good when no one sees. God sees.
9. **Correct Quietly** – When possible, handle conflicts privately, not publicly.
10. **Celebrate Honesty** – Reward truth-telling in your organization.

Questions for Reflection

1. Am I the same person in private that I am in public?
2. Where have I prioritized image over integrity?

3. What small compromises am I tolerating?
4. Who holds me accountable?
5. How do I respond when I'm caught in a mistake?
6. Would God trust me with more based on my current character?
7. What steps can I take to rebuild trust if it's been broken?

Activation: Private Audit

This week, schedule 30 minutes of quiet reflection. Ask the Holy Spirit to reveal areas of hidden compromise.

- Write down any places where your public image doesn't match your private obedience.
- Confess those areas to God.
- If needed, confess to a mentor or accountability partner.
- Commit to one visible act of integrity this week that costs you something—but honors God.

Then write out a declaration: "I choose integrity over image. I will be the same person in every room, in every season, for the glory of God."

Take it a step further: Ask three trusted people this week to describe your character. Compare their feedback with your own self-assessment and take action on any gaps.

Final Thoughts

Image may open doors, but only integrity will keep them open. In a world full of filters, may you be found faithful. In a culture chasing applause, may you chase after truth.

Integrity isn't glamorous—but it's godly. It won't always be celebrated—but it will always be rewarded. The more you cultivate it, the more God can entrust to you.

Let your yes be yes. Let your no be no. Let your life speak louder than your marketing.

Because in the Kingdom, character counts. And when integrity becomes your brand, Heaven backs your business.

Closing Prayer

Lord, search my heart and reveal any area where I've compromised integrity for image. I repent for any ways I've prioritized perception over truth. Help me to be the same person in every setting—faithful, honest, and pure before You.

Give me the courage to do what's right, even when it's hard. Strengthen my character so that my platform doesn't outgrow my foundation. Help me walk securely in Your ways, knowing that You see and reward those who live with integrity.

Make me a leader You can trust. Make me a builder who honors You in every blueprint and every decision. Let my life reflect Your truth.

In Jesus' name, Amen.

THE PRESSURE OF PRODUCTIVITY
1 SAMUEL 15:22

7

The Pressure of Productivity

Scripture Anchor: 1 Samuel 15:22

"But Samuel replied: 'Does the Lord
delight in burnt offerings and sacrifices
as much as in obeying the Lord?
To obey is better than sacrifice,
and to heed is better than the fat of rams.'"

In a culture that prizes hustle, connections, and the next big break, it's tempting to chase every opportunity that looks good on the surface. But in the Kingdom of God, not every open door is a divine invitation. Success without surrender is sabotage in disguise. The question is not, "Is this a good opportunity?" but "Is this a God opportunity?"

This chapter is about choosing obedience over ambition, direction over distraction. Because one "yes" to God's voice is more powerful than a thousand unsubmitted options. It's a call to resist the pressure of productivity and instead pursue precision in following God's path. God isn't interested in how fast you run if you're running in the wrong direction. Obedience reorients our success compass toward Heaven.

The Temptation of Opportunity

Opportunity is seductive. It appeals to our desire for influence, income, and recognition. It promises results and validation. And yet, opportunity without divine instruction can lead us far from purpose.

In entrepreneurship, opportunities abound: investors, partnerships, speaking engagements, joint ventures. The problem isn't the abundance—it's the assumption that every open door is meant to be walked through.

We often confuse movement with progress and visibility with validation. But busyness doesn't equal fruitfulness. In God's Kingdom, obedience is the only metric that matters. It's possible to have incredible opportunities and still be out of alignment.

Chasing every opportunity can dilute your energy and distort your purpose. Sometimes, the most spiritual thing you can say is "No." A focused leader is a fruitful one.

Obedience filters your decisions not through popularity or potential, but through purpose. When God is truly

Lord over your business, you no longer have the right to say "yes" without His confirmation.

Deep Dive: Saul's Disobedience and the Cost of Partial Obedience

In 1 Samuel 15, Saul is given a direct command: destroy everything belonging to the Amalekites. But Saul rationalizes, deciding to spare the best livestock and King Agag. He frames his disobedience as devotion, claiming he wanted to sacrifice the animals to the Lord.

Samuel's response is piercing: "To obey is better than sacrifice." God was not impressed with Saul's rationale. Partial obedience is still disobedience. Saul's choice to prioritize strategy over surrender cost him the kingdom.

This story is a mirror for modern leaders. How often do we justify disobedience in the name of productivity? How often do we delay or modify God's instructions because we think we know better?

Obedience is not just about what we do—it's about how we do it. God cares about the details. He cares about our posture. And He cannot bless what He didn't birth.

Saul's leadership demise reminds us that even anointed leaders can forfeit their assignment if they consistently substitute obedience for outcomes. No title or track record can exempt us from the need to listen and obey.

Had Saul obeyed fully, his legacy might have looked entirely different. Instead, God tore the kingdom from his hands and gave it to David—a man after God's own heart, a man who repented when corrected.

Obedience as a Kingdom Growth Strategy

In business, we're taught to move fast, capitalize quickly, and pivot constantly. But Kingdom entrepreneurs are called to move at the speed of God's voice. Sometimes He says, "Go." Other times, "Wait." Occasionally, "Stop."

Obedience slows you down long enough to hear divine strategy. It filters opportunities through a Kingdom lens.

Examples:

- God may tell you to walk away from a profitable client because of values misalignment.
- He might lead you to delay a launch, even when everything is ready.
- He could call you to serve in obscurity, when influence is being offered.

These decisions don't always make sense. But God sees the full picture. And when you follow Him in obedience, He gives you results that strategy alone could never produce.

Obedience is not stagnation—it's strategic alignment. It multiplies impact with less hustle because it flows from divine wisdom, not just human effort.

We are not called to be opportunity chasers; we are called to be voice followers. When you obey the whisper of the Holy Spirit, you position your business and leadership under the covering of God's authority.

The Danger of Success Without Surrender

Success is one of the greatest threats to obedience. When things are working, we assume God is blessing them. But the fruit of a season doesn't always indicate faithfulness.

Solomon, the wisest man to ever live, eventually compromised his obedience by marrying foreign women and allowing idol worship. His kingdom was vast, but his heart strayed. He ended strong in wealth but weak in worship.

This is why we must continually ask, "God, am I still in step with You?" Obedience is not a one-time decision—it's a daily discipline. It's not about perfection, but it is about surrender.

The danger of unchecked success is that it creates a false sense of invincibility. You begin to think you can maintain blessing without obedience. But in the Kingdom, the blessing follows the instruction.

Biblical Examples of Obedient Detours

- **Joseph**: Could have slept with Potiphar's wife and advanced quickly. He chose obedience and was imprisoned—but eventually elevated.
- **Jesus**: Could have avoided the cross, but submitted to the Father's will. His obedience purchased salvation for all.

- **Paul**: Obeyed the Spirit's redirection, even when it changed his ministry route (Acts 16:6–10).
- **Ananias**: Obeyed the Lord and prayed for Saul, a persecutor of Christians. His obedience helped unlock Paul's destiny.
- **Philip**: Was led away from a revival to a desert road to meet one Ethiopian eunuch. His obedience brought the Gospel to Africa.

God's path rarely looks like ours, but it always leads to purpose. Obedience protects you from premature elevation and misaligned connections.

Obedience in Modern Business Culture

In the boardroom, obedience may look like integrity in negotiations, transparency with stakeholders, or turning down money that comes with strings.

It might look like:

- Rejecting a speaking engagement because of misaligned values.
- Saying no to a partnership that compromises your mission.
- Refusing to overprice services just because competitors do.
- Not compromising Sabbath rest for short-term productivity gains.

Obedience means you stop measuring success by culture's scoreboard and start measuring it by Heaven's standard: faithfulness.

Kingdom leaders build with eternity in mind. Their goal isn't applause—it's alignment.

Practical Ways to Prioritize Obedience

1. **Write Down Instructions** – Keep a running list of what God has told you. Review it often.
2. **Discern Your Season** – Ask God what season you're in: planting, watering, harvesting, or resting?
3. **Create a Decision Filter** – Evaluate every new opportunity through prayer, counsel, Scripture, and peace.
4. **Establish Non-Negotiables** – What values won't you compromise for growth?
5. **Submit Your Plans** – As Proverbs 16:3 says, "Commit to the Lord whatever you do, and He will establish your plans."
6. **Say No Without Guilt** – Every "yes" to God requires a "no" to something else.
7. **Check for Peace** – Peace is a signal. If your spirit is unsettled, pause before proceeding.
8. **Guard Against Idolatry** – Don't confuse good things for God things. Opportunity can't replace obedience.
9. **Revisit Past Victories** – Let former faith-stories fuel your current faith-steps.
10. **Celebrate Obedience** – Acknowledge and document moments when God honored your surrender.

Questions for Reflection

1. Have I said yes to something that God never told me to pursue?
2. Am I confusing momentum with obedience?
3. What instruction have I delayed acting on?
4. Do I trust God enough to walk away from what looks good but isn't God?
5. What does success look like if God is the only audience?
6. Where have I allowed fear of missing out to override faith?
7. Am I willing to look foolish for obeying God?
8. What new level of impact might be on the other side of obedience?

Activation: The Obedience Tracker

This week, revisit your journal, prayer notes, or business goals. Identify:

- One instruction God gave that you haven't completed.
- One opportunity you've pursued without confirmation.
- One area where you need to surrender control.

Then:

- Commit to completing the instruction.
- Prayerfully release the unconfirmed opportunity.
- Write a prayer of surrender, inviting God to redirect your path.

Ask a trusted mentor to follow up with you by the end of the week.

Bonus: Identify a time in your past when you obeyed God and saw His faithfulness. Write a short testimony and share it with someone who needs encouragement. Let your past obedience remind you of God's reliability.

Final Thoughts

Obedience is not glamorous. It rarely goes viral. But it is sacred. And it is powerful. God honors the obedient. He blesses the faithful. He expands those who submit.

You don't need every open door. You only need the ones God designed for you. And when you walk in them, you'll find favor, fulfillment, and fruit that lasts.

Don't chase opportunity—chase obedience. Because when you walk with God, He will take you places you never imagined.

Obedience may cost you something in the short term, but it will secure something eternal in the long term. It is the currency of promotion in the Kingdom.

When you build your life and business on obedience, you may not always be the fastest, but you'll always be on track.

Closing Prayer

Father, thank You for reminding me that obedience is better than opportunity. Forgive me for the times I've run ahead of You, trusting my plans over Your voice. Today, I realign my heart with Your will.

Help me to discern the difference between good and God. Teach me to trust Your timing and direction, even when it doesn't make sense. Give me the faith to walk away from what looks promising if it means staying in Your will.

I surrender every ambition, every decision, and every opportunity to You. Lead me. Correct me. Protect me from distractions. Let obedience be the path I choose, not just occasionally, but daily.

And when obedience costs me something, remind me that You are worth everything. Let my legacy be defined by surrender, and let my reward be Your "well done."

In Jesus' name, Amen.

THE BLESSING OF BOUNDARIES
PROVERBS 25:28

8

The Blessing of Boundaries

Scripture Anchor: Proverbs 25:28

"Like a city whose walls are broken through
is a person who lacks self-control."

In Kingdom business, boundaries are not barriers to success—they're bridges to sustained obedience, peace, and purpose. Boundaries preserve vision, protect energy, and position leaders to operate in divine alignment rather than human exhaustion. They are not restrictive; they are deeply restorative. They enable us to operate with clarity, peace, and precision.

This chapter explores how godly boundaries can become sacred tools for stewardship—of your time, your team, your health, and your heart. Without them, the very blessings of God can become burdens.

The Purpose of Boundaries

Boundaries are not about limitation—they're about protection. They help define what is yours to carry and what is not. In leadership and business, lack of boundaries leads to burnout, blurred roles, broken relationships, and missed assignments.

God Himself modeled boundaries. He created day and night, seasons, and the Sabbath. He gave Adam responsibility over the garden but drew a line around the Tree of Knowledge. Boundaries are baked into creation—they are divine structures for order, clarity, and flourishing.

Even Jesus respected time and space. He retreated. He paused. He didn't let the crowd dictate His pace. Boundaries were woven into the rhythm of His life, and they must be in ours as well.

Without boundaries, even good things can become overwhelming. Vision turns into chaos. Hustle replaces health. And obedience becomes optional when everything is urgent. Boundaries give your yes power because they require you to say no more often.

A leader without boundaries is like a house without a roof—exposed to every storm and vulnerable to collapse.

Boundaries also affirm your identity. When you define what you say yes and no to, you reinforce who you are and what you've been called to steward.

Deep Dive: Moses and the Leadership Burden

One of the clearest examples of the importance of boundaries in leadership comes from the life of Moses. In Exodus 18, Moses is overwhelmed by the task of judging and guiding the people of Israel. From morning until evening, the people came to him with disputes, questions, and problems. He was the only point of access for the entire nation.

Moses was burning out. Though his intentions were noble, his approach was unsustainable.

Enter Jethro, his father-in-law. After observing Moses' daily grind, Jethro offered wise counsel: "What you are doing is not good... You and these people who come to you will only wear yourselves out. The work is too heavy for you; you cannot handle it alone" (Exodus 18:17–18).

Jethro encouraged Moses to delegate—to appoint capable, trustworthy leaders to oversee groups of thousands, hundreds, fifties, and tens. Only the most difficult cases were to be brought to Moses himself.

This moment marked a powerful shift in Moses' leadership. By creating boundaries, he not only protected himself from burnout, but he also empowered others to lead and grow.

Moses learned that saying no to everything didn't mean failure—it meant faithfulness. Boundaries preserved his longevity and increased his effectiveness.

The lesson? Leadership without limits leads to loss. But boundaries multiply both impact and capacity.

Boundaries and Self-Control

Proverbs 25:28 compares a person without self-control to a city with broken-down walls. In ancient times, a city's strength was measured by its walls. Without them, it was exposed, weak, and defenseless.

The same is true in leadership. Without boundaries, leaders overextend, overcommit, and operate from depletion. They lose clarity, creativity, and character.

Self-control is the gatekeeper of healthy boundaries. It enables you to:

- Stop working when it's time to rest.
- Say no without guilt.
- Disconnect without apology.
- Prioritize what God has asked over what people expect.

Self-control doesn't just protect your schedule—it protects your soul. It keeps you aligned with God's priorities and guards you from people-pleasing, perfectionism, and pride.

Boundaries rooted in self-control don't push people away—they pull priorities into proper alignment. A boundary-less life is one governed by reaction rather than intention.

Why Leaders Resist Boundaries

Many leaders associate boundaries with restriction. They fear saying no will mean missed opportunities or disappointed people. But the opposite is true—clear boundaries build trust and increase impact.

Common resistance sounds like:

- "If I don't do it, who will?"
- "I'll rest after the next big project."
- "I can't afford to say no."

These thoughts stem from a scarcity mindset. But in the Kingdom, obedience trumps busyness, and rest is a form of worship. When you set boundaries, you declare that your source is God, not your grind.

Boundaries also create space for others to rise. When you let go of what's not yours, others have room to grow in their own calling. Delegation is a form of discipleship.

True leadership is not about doing everything—it's about doing the right things and helping others do the same.

We also resist boundaries because we've tied our identity to our productivity. But God defines us by who we are in Him, not what we do for Him. Boundaries remind us we are loved, even when we're offline.

Boundaries in Business

1. **Time Boundaries** – Set work hours and honor Sabbath. Don't let urgency rob your rest.
2. **Relational Boundaries** – Don't hire friends or family without clear agreements. Guard emotional energy.
3. **Financial Boundaries** – Tithe first. Budget wisely. Say no to offers that compromise values.
4. **Mission Boundaries** – Stay focused on your God-given lane. Don't chase every trend.
5. **Emotional Boundaries** – Don't absorb everyone's problems. You are not the Savior.
6. **Team Boundaries** – Define roles, responsibilities, and expectations clearly.
7. **Mental Boundaries** – Guard your thought life. Refuse to meditate on lies or people-pleasing.
8. **Digital Boundaries** – Limit screen time. Schedule "offline" hours.

Clear boundaries create healthy culture. They establish mutual respect and foster longevity. Without them, toxicity grows, roles blur, and burnout becomes inevitable.

Boundaries not only define what is permissible—they also define what is possible. They make room for creativity, innovation, margin, and peace.

Boundaries and Rest

God rested—not because He was tired, but because He was modeling wholeness. Sabbath is not about inactivity—it's about intentional reset. It's a boundary that says, "I trust God to sustain what I release."

Rest is obedience. Leaders who rest regularly lead better, think clearer, love deeper, and endure longer.

Without boundaries for rest:

- Creativity suffers.
- Relationships deteriorate.
- Spiritual sensitivity dulls.

Rest restores your soul, renews your vision, and reaffirms your dependency on God. Regular rest is not laziness—it's leadership. It reminds you that you are not God, and that your work does not define your worth.

Sabbath is not weakness—it's warfare. It's your resistance to the idolatry of productivity.

When you honor rest, you're telling God, "I trust You to finish what I cannot." That's not lazy—it's leadership aligned with Heaven.

Jesus Modeled Boundaries

Jesus often withdrew from the crowds to pray. He didn't heal everyone, respond to every request, or explain His every move. He lived with divine boundaries.

- When crowds grew, He retreated to solitude.
- When criticized, He responded with silence or truth.
- When tempted, He quoted Scripture and stayed anchored.

He was Spirit-led, not demand-driven.

As His followers, we are invited to do the same—to discern what is ours to carry, when to say yes, and when to walk away. Following Jesus includes following His example of sacred margin.

You don't have to be everything to everyone. You have to be obedient to the One.

If Jesus—the Savior of the world—needed boundaries to sustain His mission, how much more do we?

Practical Ways to Establish Boundaries

1. **Define Your Priorities** – What has God called you to steward in this season?
2. **Schedule Your Values** – Put rest, prayer, and family on the calendar first.
3. **Use "No" as a Tool** – Say it with grace and without guilt.
4. **Block Time for Deep Work** – Protect your most productive hours from interruptions.
5. **Communicate Expectations** – With your team, clients, and loved ones.
6. **Turn Off Notifications** – Reclaim your attention. Presence is power.
7. **Ask for Accountability** – Let someone help you uphold your limits.
8. **Honor the Sabbath** – Choose one day a week to stop striving and enjoy God.
9. **Review Your Boundaries Monthly** – Seasons change; so should your limits.

10. **Celebrate Small Wins** – Every time you honor a boundary, you honor God.

Questions for Reflection

1. Where in my life have I allowed walls to break down?
2. What commitments are draining my energy without aligning with my assignment?
3. Do I honor my need for rest, or do I glorify busyness?
4. What relationships or responsibilities need clearer boundaries?
5. How might boundaries improve my leadership, creativity, and peace?
6. What fear keeps me from establishing firm boundaries?
7. Who do I need to have a boundary-setting conversation with this week?
8. What is one area where I need to say no so I can say yes to God?

Activation: Build the Wall

This week, identify one area where a boundary is needed.

1. Write down the boundary you will establish.
2. Set a date and time to implement it.
3. Communicate it clearly to those it affects.
4. Track how your peace, energy, or productivity shifts.
5. Thank God for helping you build healthy walls.

Bonus Challenge: Choose one day to fully unplug from work. Reflect on how it impacts your spirit, body, and creativity. Then journal what God showed you during that time.

Final Thoughts

Boundaries are not selfish—they are sacred. They protect what God has given and position you to flourish in your calling. They teach others how to treat you, and they teach your soul how to rest.

God cannot bless what you do not protect. When you build healthy walls around your time, heart, and energy, you are creating space for sustainable obedience.

You were not created to carry everything. You were created to carry what God assigns. Let boundaries be the blueprint that honors both your calling and your Creator.

Boundaries are one of the most radical acts of trust you can practice in leadership. They say, "God, I trust You enough to rest. I believe You can handle what I release." That trust opens the door to supernatural peace.

In a world addicted to access and performance, let your boundaries be a prophetic statement: "I belong to God, not the grind."

Closing Prayer

Father, thank You for the gift of boundaries. Thank You for modeling rest, rhythm, and self-control. Forgive me for the times I've overcommitted, overextended, or tried to please people more than I honored You.

Help me build healthy boundaries that reflect Your wisdom and protect what You've entrusted to me. Give me courage to say no when needed, and discernment to know what belongs on my plate.

Teach me to lead with margin, rest with joy, and serve from overflow. May my boundaries reflect trust in You, not fear of missing out.

Help me to value purpose over pressure, and obedience over busyness. Strengthen my walls, O Lord, so that I may lead from a place of peace. Empower me to create rhythms that reflect Your Kingdom, not the culture. Let my leadership be both fruitful and full of rest.

In Jesus' name, Amen.

PROSPERITY WITH PURPOSE
DEUTERONOMY 8:18

9

Prosperity with Purpose

Scripture Anchor: Deuteronomy 8:18

"But remember the Lord your God,
for it is He who gives you the ability to produce wealth,
and so confirms His covenant, which He swore
to your ancestors, as it is today."

In the Kingdom, wealth is never an end—it's a means. Prosperity isn't about flaunting success but fulfilling purpose. God gives us the ability to produce wealth not just to bless us, but to bless others, fund His mission, and confirm His covenant on earth.

This chapter explores what it means to pursue prosperity with Kingdom purpose, grounding your financial life in obedience, impact, and eternal legacy. We will dive into the life of Abraham—blessed beyond measure, yet anchored by his unwavering commitment to follow God's voice.

Prosperity with Kingdom Perspective

Too often, prosperity is either idolized or ignored. The world chases wealth for status and self-gratification. Meanwhile, many in the church shy away from money out of fear or false humility. But neither extreme reflects God's heart.

Kingdom prosperity is about stewardship, not status. It's about living in abundance for the purpose of overflow—so that God's mission can move forward and others can flourish. The blessing is never meant to stop with us. It's designed to flow through us.

Deuteronomy 8:18 reminds us that it is God who gives us the power to get wealth. That means our intellect, skills, creativity, and business opportunities are divine deposits. We don't create success—we steward what God enables.

When you understand this, money becomes a tool, not a trophy. It becomes a resource for Kingdom advancement, not personal elevation.

When business owners and leaders shift from ownership to stewardship, their definition of success changes. They begin asking, "How can I use this blessing to meet needs beyond my own? What eternal fruit can grow from this resource?"

Deep Dive: Abraham—Prosperity Anchored in Purpose

Abraham is one of the most prominent examples of prosperity with purpose. In Genesis 12:2–3, God tells him, "I will bless you...and all peoples on earth will be blessed through you." From the beginning, Abraham's blessing had a mission attached to it.

He became extremely wealthy—livestock, silver, gold, land, and influence. Yet at every turn, Abraham demonstrated that his trust was in God, not his assets. When Lot's herdsmen quarreled with his, Abraham gave Lot the first choice of land, trusting that God's promise wasn't tied to territory but to obedience (Genesis 13).

In Genesis 14, Abraham refuses to take plunder from the king of Sodom after rescuing Lot, saying, "I will accept nothing belonging to you...so that you will never be able to say, 'I made Abram rich'" (v. 23). Abraham didn't need a king's favor—he had God's.

Then in Genesis 22, Abraham faces his greatest test. God asks him to sacrifice Isaac, the very son of the promise. Abraham obeys, and God provides a ram. This moment not only cements Abraham's legacy of faith—it unlocks a generational blessing. "Because you have done this...I will surely bless you...and through your offspring all nations on earth will be blessed" (Genesis 22:16–18).

Abraham's life proves this: the truly prosperous are those who obey God fully and steward their resources with open hands.

His prosperity didn't come from manipulation, exploitation, or shortcuts—it came from covenant. It came from a lifestyle of obedience and faith.

Abraham also built altars—symbols of worship, honor, and thanksgiving. Every time God advanced him, Abraham responded with worship. In the same way, we must remember that prosperity is not just a sign of progress, but an opportunity for praise.

Misconceptions About Wealth

There are several common misconceptions about wealth in the Kingdom:

- **Misconception #1: Money is evil.** Truth: Money is neutral. It's a tool. The love of money is the root of evil (1 Timothy 6:10), not money itself.
- **Misconception #2: Poverty is more spiritual.** Truth: Jesus became poor so that we might be rich (2 Corinthians 8:9). The goal isn't poverty—it's generosity and obedience.
- **Misconception #3: If I make more, I'll become greedy.** Truth: Money doesn't change you—it magnifies you. More resources amplify the heart posture you already have.
- **Misconception #4: Prosperity is about lavish living.** Truth: Prosperity in God's eyes is about fullness and flow—not hoarding, but releasing. It includes peace, purpose, and provision for every good work.

- **Misconception #5: Prosperity is only financial.** Truth: Biblical prosperity includes health, favor, fruitfulness, joy, and alignment. It's holistic.

These lies keep believers small. But God desires His people to walk in abundance—not to hoard it, but to release it for Kingdom impact.

Why God Gives Wealth

Deuteronomy 8:18 says God gives the ability to produce wealth to confirm His covenant. That means your business success isn't just a blessing—it's a signal to the world that God keeps His promises.

Wealth in the hands of the righteous is a weapon for righteousness:

- It funds ministry.
- It breaks generational curses.
- It creates employment and dignity.
- It transforms communities.
- It answers prayer requests.
- It equips others to fulfill their God-given purpose.

You're not called to chase wealth. You're called to steward it. Prosperity is a divine trust.

God's wealth has a mission. If we treat it like a status symbol, we waste it. If we treat it like a resource, we multiply it.

The church is waking up to its financial calling—not just to be recipients of blessing, but to be financiers of

Kingdom advancement. That's what happens when prosperity is coupled with purpose.

Practical Ways to Prosper with Purpose

1. **Tithe Faithfully** – Give God your first fruits, not your leftovers. This cultivates humility and trust.
2. **Give Generously** – Build a lifestyle of radical generosity. Plan for giving, not just spending. Make giving a monthly line item.
3. **Budget Prayerfully** – Don't just track dollars—assign them mission. Ask the Holy Spirit to guide your financial decisions.
4. **Invest Strategically** – Look for businesses, causes, and ventures that align with Kingdom values. Your investments can influence culture.
5. **Live Below Your Means** – Simplicity creates margin. Margin funds mission. Extravagance without purpose is a distraction.
6. **Teach Financial Stewardship** – Multiply wisdom by mentoring others. Equip others to manage what God has given them.
7. **Create Job Opportunities** – Build businesses that empower people and restore dignity. Job creation is one of the most tangible ways to fulfill your calling.
8. **Support Kingdom Work** – Partner financially with ministries, missions, and movements. Become an answered prayer for someone else.
9. **Honor Financial Covenants** – Pay debts with integrity. Honor your word in financial matters.

10. **Plan for Legacy** – Create a vision for what your wealth will accomplish beyond your lifetime. Fund future impact.
11. **Balance Saving with Sowing** – Build wise reserves, but don't withhold when God prompts you to give.
12. **Measure Impact, Not Just Income** – Evaluate success by lives changed, not dollars earned.

Questions for Reflection

1. Do I see my ability to produce wealth as a divine gift?
2. How is my prosperity currently impacting others?
3. Have I made money a source instead of a tool?
4. What would radical generosity look like in this season?
5. Is my financial strategy aligned with my faith?
6. Who is being transformed because I steward well?
7. What financial boundaries do I need to implement to stay in obedience?
8. If God doubled my resources tomorrow, what would change—and what wouldn't?
9. Is my giving a reflection of worship, or obligation?
10. What story do I want my finances to tell when I'm gone?

Activation: Prosperity Audit

This week, take an honest look at your finances:

- Review your income, giving, saving, and spending.
- Identify areas where God has increased you.
- Ask: "Where am I prospering without purpose?"

- Choose one new way to align your prosperity with God's priorities.

Write a financial mission statement—why you earn, give, invest, and spend. Let it guide your next decision.

Next, select one tangible act of generosity you can practice this week. Whether it's blessing a family, funding a cause, or sowing into someone's dream—act on it quickly.

Then journal about the experience. How did it shift your perspective? What did it reveal about your relationship with money and mission?

Talk with your spouse, mentor, or accountability partner about your vision for financial stewardship. Invite feedback and prayer.

Final Thoughts

God has no issue with you prospering—He just doesn't want prosperity to become your god. When your heart is aligned and your hands are open, He can trust you with more.

Prosperity with purpose changes the world. It funds dreams, plants churches, heals communities, and lifts the oppressed. And it all starts with obedience.

Abraham didn't chase riches. He followed God—and the riches followed. May that be said of you.

Wealth without wisdom is waste. But prosperity anchored in purpose is fuel for transformation. You are not just building a portfolio—you're building legacy.

Let your success point to the Source. Let your prosperity preach a sermon of faith, stewardship, and Kingdom vision.

Live and give in a way that makes Heaven proud.

Closing Prayer

Father, thank You for giving me the ability to produce wealth. I recognize that every opportunity, idea, and provision comes from You. Help me to steward what I have with wisdom, faith, and a heart for impact.

Protect me from the trap of greed, the fear of lack, and the pride of ownership. Align my heart with Yours. Teach me to prosper with purpose—to give generously, invest wisely, and build for eternity.

May my business reflect Your glory and my finances fuel Your mission. Let every dollar be a disciple, every investment an act of faith, and every return a testimony to Your goodness.

Let my prosperity declare Your faithfulness. Let my stewardship reflect Your Kingdom.

Show me how to be a vessel of provision for others. Let my giving restore hope, rebuild dreams, and resource destiny.

In Jesus' name, Amen.

ANOINTED FOR ADVERSITY
2 CORINTHIANS 12:9-10

10

Anointed for Adversity

Scripture Anchor: 2 Corinthians 12:9–10

"But he said to me, 'My grace is sufficient for you, for my power is made perfect in weakness.' Therefore I will boast all the more gladly about my weaknesses, so that Christ's power may rest on me. That is why, for Christ's sake, I delight in weaknesses, in insults, in hardships, in persecutions, in difficulties. For when I am weak, then I am strong."

Adversity is not a detour from your destiny—it's often the proving ground for it. In Kingdom business, challenges are not signs of failure but signals of preparation. God doesn't waste pain; He repurposes it for power. While the world may see adversity as a sign to quit, Kingdom leaders understand it as an invitation to go deeper into purpose.

This chapter explores how to navigate opposition, resistance, and hardship through the lens of faith. Anchored in the story of the Apostle Paul, we will see how adversity can become a platform for greater authority, grace, and impact. Whether you're dealing with financial loss, betrayal, delayed dreams, or leadership pressures, this chapter will remind you that you are not disqualified—you're being developed.

God's Grace Is Built for the Battle

As believers in the marketplace, we often pray for favor, but what we receive is fire. We pray for opportunity, but encounter opposition. This doesn't mean God is absent—it means He's training us. Just like muscle is built through tension, faith is developed through adversity.

Paul, one of the most anointed leaders in Scripture, wrote more than half of the New Testament while enduring shipwrecks, beatings, imprisonment, and betrayal. And yet, his most profound revelation wasn't about theology—it was about grace.

In 2 Corinthians 12, Paul pleads with God to remove a "thorn in the flesh." God doesn't grant his request. Instead, He responds with, "My grace is sufficient for you, for my power is made perfect in weakness."

This is a Kingdom paradox: our greatest strength is found in our surrender. Our breakthrough doesn't come from control—it comes from consecration. You are not strong because of your credentials. You are strong because of your connection to Christ.

The grace of God isn't just to escape adversity—it's to endure it with purpose. It empowers us to move forward when our natural capacity is depleted. His grace bridges the gap between where we are and where He is calling us.

Adversity Is a Setup for Assignment

We often want elevation without agitation. But in the Kingdom, elevation comes through endurance. Every God-given assignment attracts adversity because the enemy opposes what brings God glory.

Adversity is not proof that you missed God—it's often evidence that you're right on schedule. Consider Joseph. He dreamed of leadership, but was sold into slavery, falsely accused, and imprisoned. Yet every setback was a step toward his assignment to lead Egypt.

Adversity isn't the absence of God's plan—it's often the path to it. It teaches us to lead not with pride, but with perspective. It builds the character necessary to sustain the calling.

When adversity arises in business—whether through rejection, failure, betrayal, or burnout—it is not the end. It may actually be the moment God chooses to refine your vision, realign your focus, and reaffirm your mission.

Paul himself experienced adversity at nearly every turn:

- He was rejected by the very church he sought to serve.
- He was shipwrecked while pursuing his mission.
- He was stoned and left for dead while preaching the gospel.

Yet he kept going. Why? Because he understood that adversity was not the enemy—it was the anointing's training ground. It refined his motives, clarified his mission, and multiplied his message.

What if the struggle you're facing right now is actually preparing you for supernatural strategy?

The Anointing Isn't Just for Comfort—It's for Confrontation

The anointing is not just about goosebumps and good feelings. It's divine empowerment for divine assignment. And that includes the courage to confront hard things.

David was anointed long before he sat on a throne. But between the anointing and the crown came a giant, a jealous king, caves, and countless battles. His anointing didn't eliminate adversity—it attracted it.

But every battle David faced refined his character. Every trial taught him how to lead, love, and lean on God. When you are truly anointed, you don't run from adversity—you rise through it.

You become stronger in storms. Your prayers deepen in pressure. Your vision sharpens in valleys.

The same God who anoints you for success also anoints you for suffering—not because He enjoys your pain, but because He's committed to your purpose.

Many are called to platforms, but few are willing to carry the process. Don't despise the press—it's the path to power.

Deep Dive: Paul's Endurance and Eternal Impact

Paul's entire ministry was marked by hardship. In 2 Corinthians 11:23–28, he lists beatings, imprisonments, lashes, danger, hunger, sleepless nights, and more. He was no stranger to adversity. Yet he wrote, "I delight in weaknesses… for when I am weak, then I am strong."

This wasn't denial—it was divine insight. Paul saw trials not as setbacks, but as setups. Every difficulty refined his calling and expanded his reach.

Paul's strength didn't come from avoiding adversity. It came from embracing grace in the midst of it. And that grace became the fuel for his mission.

Even in chains, Paul wrote letters that continue to transform lives today. His adversity birthed legacy.

His prison became his pulpit. His scars became sermons. His setbacks became supernatural setups.

Likewise, your most difficult seasons may produce your most powerful contributions. Your business testimony, your resilience, your creative breakthrough—they are all forged in the fire of adversity.

What Adversity Produces in You

1. **Resilience** – The ability to bounce back stronger.
2. **Empathy** – A heart that understands the pain of others.
3. **Wisdom** – Insight forged through experience.
4. **Dependence** – A deeper reliance on the Holy Spirit.
5. **Authority** – Spiritual weight that comes from surviving what others didn't.
6. **Focus** – Clarity about what truly matters.
7. **Creativity** – Innovation born from constraint.
8. **Prayer Life** – An unshakable communion with God.
9. **Endurance** – A spirit that keeps going when others would quit.
10. **Compassion** – A leadership style shaped by service, not self.
11. **Character** – Integrity that stands even when it's hard.
12. **Testimony** – Evidence of God's power working through you.

God never allows adversity to break you—only to shape you.

Leading Through Adversity in Business

1. **Anchor in Identity** – Remember who you are in Christ, not just what you do.
2. **Lean into Community** – Don't isolate. Invite trusted voices into your process.

3. **Pause Before You Pivot** – Resist making fear-based decisions.
4. **Ask the Right Questions** – Not "Why me?" but "What is God forming in me?"
5. **Stay Spirit-Led** – Keep prayer at the center of every strategic move.
6. **Lead with Transparency** – Share lessons with your team. Vulnerability builds trust.
7. **Use Your Testimony** – Your breakthrough can be someone else's blueprint.
8. **Train Through Trials** – Let adversity become a curriculum for future leaders.
9. **Rest in the Process** – Don't rush resurrection. Jesus spent three days in the tomb.
10. **Speak Life Daily** – Declare what God says, not what fear whispers.
11. **Celebrate Small Wins** – In adversity, progress is still progress.

Questions for Reflection

1. Where am I facing adversity right now?
2. How might God be using this hardship to strengthen me?
3. Am I trying to escape the process or embrace the grace?
4. What past trial became a foundation for future success?
5. Who needs to hear the testimony of how I overcame?

6. What spiritual discipline has adversity deepened in my life?
7. How has adversity clarified my calling?
8. Do I believe God is still working, even when I don't feel it?
9. What area of my leadership is being refined by pressure?
10. Am I allowing adversity to draw me closer to God or push me further from Him?
11. What internal shift has taken place because of external hardship?
12. What Scripture sustains me when my strength feels gone?

Activation: Name the Grace in the Grind

This week, identify one area of adversity in your life or business. Write out:

- The challenge.
- The emotion it stirs.
- The lesson it's teaching.
- The grace God is showing.

Then, write a short prayer or affirmation that declares God's sufficiency in that area. Speak it daily.

Also, reach out to someone walking through a tough time. Share part of your journey to encourage them. Let your testimony be their turning point.

As an added step, create a "Faith Under Fire" journal. Document how God meets you in adversity. Over time, you'll have a record of His faithfulness to reflect on when future challenges arise.

Write down three moments in your past when you thought you wouldn't make it—but did. Use them as reminders that God hasn't failed you yet.

Final Thoughts

You are not just surviving adversity—you are being shaped by it. God is forging endurance, sharpening vision, and preparing you for weightier assignments.

The anointing isn't just for platform—it's for pressure. It enables you to stand when others fall, to sing when others sink, to build when others break.

Paul learned that strength isn't found in self—it's found in surrender. Your greatest power may come from the places that once felt like your greatest pain.

You are anointed for adversity.

Not to avoid it. Not to be crushed by it. But to rise through it—with grace, grit, and God's glory on your life.

Let every trial train you. Let every hardship humble you. Let every valley reveal the God who walks with you.

You don't need the absence of adversity—you need the awareness of the Anointed One who walks with you through it.

Closing Prayer

Father, thank You for trusting me with adversity. Thank You that Your grace is sufficient and Your power is made perfect in my weakness. Help me not to fear hardship but to embrace Your strength within it.

Teach me to lead with resilience, to endure with faith, and to rise with joy even in the midst of storms. Let my adversity produce endurance, character, and hope.

Give me eyes to see purpose in the pressure and strength to persevere when it feels like too much. Remind me that I'm not walking through this alone—that You go before me, beside me, and within me.

Make me anointed for adversity—not for my glory, but for Yours. Let every trial become a testimony. Let every weakness point to Your strength.

Use my pain to produce purpose. Use my scars to release healing. Use my story to bring hope.

Help me to walk in grace, lead with humility, and overcome through Your power.

In Jesus' name, Amen.

SACRIFICE AS A DIVINE STRATEGY
ROMANS 12:1–2

11

Sacrifice as a Divine Strategy

Scripture Anchor: Romans 12:1–2

"Therefore, I urge you, brothers and sisters, in view of God's mercy, to offer your bodies as a living sacrifice, holy and pleasing to God—this is your true and proper worship. Do not conform to the pattern of this world, but be transformed by the renewing of your mind. Then you will be able to test and approve what God's will is—his good, pleasing and perfect will."

In Kingdom business, sacrifice is not just a spiritual discipline—it's a divine strategy. In a culture that glorifies accumulation and advancement, God calls His people to live differently: to scale through surrender and multiply through obedience. True Kingdom success does not begin with what we gain, but with what we're willing to give up.

This chapter explores how the life of a believer in business must be marked by daily sacrifice—of ego, control, comfort, and personal ambition—in order to steward God's vision with clarity, power, and purpose. Using the powerful story of the woman with the alabaster jar, we will unpack how costly acts of obedience release Kingdom-level impact.

A Life Laid Down

Romans 12:1 doesn't call for a momentary sacrifice—it calls for a lifestyle. Paul urges us to offer our very lives as living sacrifices. In business terms, this means your calendar, your conversations, your decisions, your investments—all of it—belongs on the altar.

To be a living sacrifice is to walk out your worship daily. Not in theory, but in practice. Not just in church, but in boardrooms, budgets, and brainstorming sessions.

Living sacrifice is about perpetual surrender. It's choosing submission over striving, holiness over hustle, and God's voice over the noise of the culture.

Sacrifice is not about loss—it's about love. It's about trusting that what you place in God's hands will always return greater than what you keep in your own.

It's also about stewardship. When you sacrifice your plans for God's, you steward His presence and purpose in your work. What you lay down today may open doors tomorrow you never imagined.

Deep Dive: The Alabaster Offering

In Matthew 26, a woman approached Jesus with an alabaster jar filled with expensive perfume. Without hesitation, she broke it open and poured it on Jesus' head as an act of extravagant worship. The disciples were shocked. "Why this waste?" they questioned. But Jesus responded, "She has done a beautiful thing to me."

What the world called waste, Jesus called worship.

The alabaster jar represented her most valuable possession. And she poured it out—not sparingly, not partially, but completely. She held nothing back. Her act prepared Jesus for burial and prophetically honored Him before His greatest sacrifice.

In your business, you too carry alabaster jars—things of great value that God may ask you to break open for His glory. It might be your financial margin, your intellectual property, your influence, or even a career path. But when you pour it out at His feet, He breathes on it.

And like the woman's offering, your sacrifice becomes your legacy.

Imagine the courage it took to break the jar. It was irreversible. No resealing it. No controlling the pace or portion. It was all or nothing. That's the nature of true sacrifice—it cannot be taken back. It declares total trust.

The Pattern of the World vs. the Posture of the Kingdom

Romans 12:2 reminds us not to conform to the patterns of this world. The world's pattern in business is driven by self-promotion, shortcuts, and a hunger for recognition. But the Kingdom posture is radically different. It is grounded in humility, delayed gratification, and trust in divine timing.

Worldly scale says:

- Market louder.
- Move faster.
- Control everything.

Kingdom scale says:

- Build in silence.
- Move at God's pace.
- Release what you can't control.

The world teaches that influence is achieved through charisma, control, and competition. The Kingdom teaches that influence flows through humility, service, and surrender.

This doesn't mean we reject excellence or ambition. It means we surrender our strategy to God's sovereignty. We give Him the blueprint, the budget, and the boardroom—and we trust Him with the outcome.

What Sacrifice Looks Like in Kingdom Business

1. **Obeying Promptings That Don't Make Sense** – Like launching before you're ready or giving when it feels risky.
2. **Declining Deals That Compromise Values** – Even if the money's good.
3. **Prioritizing Mission Over Metrics** – Impact before income.
4. **Letting Go of Control** – Delegating and trusting others to lead.
5. **Choosing Rest Over Hustle** – Trusting that obedience trumps output.
6. **Firing Toxic Clients or Partners** – Protecting culture over cash.
7. **Investing in People Others Overlook** – Seeing potential where others see problems.
8. **Tithing and Sowing Generously** – Not just from surplus, but from faith.
9. **Operating in Excellence When No One Is Watching** – Offering your best even when no one applauds.
10. **Staying Silent When You Want to Defend Yourself** – Trusting God to be your vindicator.

These are not one-time sacrifices. They are postures of the heart. They are what it looks like to walk as a living sacrifice in your vocation.

Sacrifice Always Precedes Multiplication

In John 12:24, Jesus said, "Unless a grain of wheat falls to the ground and dies, it remains alone. But if it dies, it produces many seeds." This is the blueprint for Kingdom growth: death before fruit, surrender before scale.

Your greatest growth may be on the other side of your greatest sacrifice.

God doesn't multiply what we withhold—He multiplies what we release. When you give up what you thought you needed, He gives back more than you imagined.

Your sacrifice becomes seed. Seed becomes harvest. And harvest becomes legacy.

What Sacrifice Produces in You

1. **Humility** – A reminder that everything is God's.
2. **Spiritual Sensitivity** – A heightened awareness of His voice.
3. **Freedom** – From fear, comparison, and performance.
4. **Obedience** – A habit of saying yes to God.
5. **Character** – Depth forged in private surrender.
6. **Kingdom Authority** – Power that flows from submission.
7. **Legacy** – A life that echoes beyond the boardroom.
8. **Peace** – The kind that comes from knowing you're in God's will.
9. **Perspective** – Understanding that eternity matters more than momentary applause.

10. **Influence** – Not built by branding, but by brokenness before God.

Reflection Questions

1. What is my alabaster jar?
2. What am I currently clinging to that God may be asking me to surrender?
3. Have I chosen comfort over calling in any area of my life or business?
4. Where have I equated sacrifice with loss instead of worship?
5. Who might be impacted by my obedience?
6. What fruit have I seen from past sacrifices?
7. Am I building for today or for eternity?
8. What does radical obedience look like for me this week?
9. How can I recalibrate my definition of success to align with Heaven?
10. Am I willing to trust God with the outcome if I give Him everything?

Activation: Sacrifice in Action

Identify one area in your life or business where God may be asking for a sacrifice. It could be time, finances, relationships, control, or reputation.

Take a bold step this week:

- Cancel a meeting to prioritize rest or family.

- Say no to an opportunity that compromises your values.
- Give generously to someone who can't repay you.
- Release a decision you've been holding onto in fear.
- Publicly honor someone you've privately envied.

Journal the experience and how God shows up. Then, share your testimony with someone who needs encouragement to obey.

Don't underestimate the power of simple obedience. It may seem small now, but it may be the first domino in a chain of eternal impact.

Final Thoughts

Sacrifice isn't about impressing God—it's about trusting Him. It's not about emptying your life—it's about making room for what only He can fill. When we live surrendered, we become candidates for supernatural scale.

The woman with the alabaster jar didn't know her story would be preached for generations. She simply obeyed. She didn't build a brand—she built an altar.

You're not called to scale like the world. You're called to scale like the Kingdom: through sacrifice, surrender, and steadfast obedience. What you lay down today becomes the seed of tomorrow's harvest.

Let your life be the jar. Let your obedience be the perfume. Let your worship fill the room.

Closing Prayer

Father, thank You for inviting me to the altar. Thank You for showing me that sacrifice is not loss but love. Teach me to trust You enough to pour out everything I've been holding back.

Break my pride. Break my need for control. And break my heart for what breaks Yours. Let every decision I make in life and business reflect surrender.

May my obedience be extravagant. May my worship be costly. And may my impact be eternal.

I give You my plans. I give You my platform. I give You my everything.

I trust that as I lay down what I cannot keep, You will give me what I could never earn.

In Jesus' name, Amen.

LEGACY THAT LASTS
PSALM 112:1–6

12

Legacy That Lasts

Scripture Anchor: Psalm 112:1–6

"Praise the Lord. Blessed are those who fear the Lord, who find great delight in his commands. Their children will be mighty in the land; the generation of the upright will be blessed. Wealth and riches are in their houses, and their righteousness endures forever. Even in darkness light dawns for the upright, for those who are gracious and compassionate and righteous. Good will come to those who are generous and lend freely, who conduct their affairs with justice. Surely the righteous will never be shaken; they will be remembered forever."

True success is not measured by what you build, but by what you leave behind. Legacy is the fruit of faithfulness—a life lived with eternity in mind. In Kingdom business, legacy is not about fame or fortune; it's about impact, integrity, and inheritance.

This chapter unpacks how lasting legacy is formed through obedience, generosity, and righteousness. We will explore David's preparation for Solomon to build the temple and how his behind-the-scenes obedience laid a foundation for generational blessing.

Living with the End in Mind

Legacy begins with perspective. If your vision ends with your lifetime, it's too small for the Kingdom. God calls us to build not just for ourselves, but for generations. Psalm 112 paints a vivid picture of generational impact: the upright person leaves behind spiritual strength, financial blessing, and a reputation that endures.

When you operate in business with legacy in mind, decisions are made differently:

- You prioritize people over profit.
- You invest in succession, not just success.
- You build structures that last beyond your leadership.
- You plant seeds that you may never see harvest.

Legacy thinking means you stop asking, "What can I gain today?" and start asking, "What will remain tomorrow?"

Imagine a business leader who walks into a meeting room, not with the intention of impressing stakeholders, but with a prayerful heart asking God how this conversation can bless generations to come. That is the legacy mindset—it sees every move not as a transaction, but as a seed.

Deep Dive: David's Preparation for Solomon

In 1 Chronicles 28–29, King David is nearing the end of his reign. His greatest desire was to build a temple for the Lord. But God tells him that Solomon, his son, will be the one to carry it out. Instead of being discouraged, David shifts from builder to preparer.

Rather than retreating in disappointment, David steps into purpose with renewed clarity. He understands that just because he will not finish the project does not mean he cannot play a part in it.

He spends the rest of his leadership not building the temple, but setting up Solomon to succeed. He gathers gold, silver, bronze, iron, wood, onyx, marble, and more. He organizes the Levites, trains leadership, and lays out the plans.

Picture David in his older age, surrounded by blueprints and resources, meeting with officials, speaking into the lives of young leaders, coaching Solomon not just as a king, but as a spiritual father. He's laying the groundwork for a temple he will never enter. And he does it joyfully.

David didn't just leave Solomon an idea—he left him infrastructure.

That is legacy. David knew the temple would outlive him. And he didn't need to see it with his own eyes to know it mattered.

Your legacy may not be the thing you build—but the people and systems you prepare to build it after you.

Characteristics of a Legacy Leader

1. **Vision Beyond Self** – You think generationally, not transactionally.
2. **Obedience Over Visibility** – You're content to do the work even if your name isn't in lights.
3. **Generosity in Private** – You sow in secret, knowing God rewards openly.
4. **Integrity in the Small Things** – You live with consistency, not compromise.
5. **Stewardship of Opportunity** – You treat every resource as something to multiply, not waste.
6. **Empowerment of Others** – You pour into people who will carry the vision forward.
7. **Faith in the Unseen** – You believe that what God starts through you will not end with you.

Legacy is not left by accident. It's built intentionally—choice by choice, day by day.

Building Legacy in Business

Legacy in business isn't just about inheritance—it's about influence. You can't control how long you live, but you can control what you live for. Here's how legacy-minded leaders operate:

- **They Document Vision** – Leaving behind clear mission and values.
- **They Build Teams, Not Just Products** – People outlast platforms.
- **They Disciple in the Marketplace** – Leadership development with a Kingdom lens.
- **They Share Wisdom Freely** – Pouring into mentees and future leaders.
- **They Create Systems for Sustainability** – Ensuring the mission can run without them.

Consider the leader who trains others to lead, who doesn't just delegate tasks but develops future decision-makers. That's legacy in action. It's not about building empires—it's about building people.

If your business dies when you step away, it wasn't legacy—it was ego. Legacy ensures that your impact continues without your presence.

What Psalm 112 Teaches Us

Psalm 112 reveals the blueprint for a lasting legacy:

- **Fear the Lord** – A life rooted in reverence for God.
- **Delight in His commands** – Loving His Word and living it out.
- **Generosity** – Giving freely and with joy.
- **Justice** – Conducting affairs with equity and righteousness.

- **Faithfulness** – A life that can't be shaken.

This is more than a eulogy. It's eternal recognition. God honors those who live to honor Him. And generations will thank you for your faithfulness.

Legacy is often built in obscurity. It's forged in early mornings of prayer, quiet moments of giving when no one sees, late nights developing systems no one claps for. But God sees. And heaven keeps record.

Reflection Questions

1. What do I want people to say about my life 50 years from now?
2. Am I building something that will outlive me?
3. Who am I preparing to carry the vision after me?
4. Where can I invest in others to ensure legacy, not just longevity?
5. What values must I codify now to ensure they continue later?
6. How am I stewarding influence beyond income?
7. What seeds can I sow now that future generations will reap?

Activation: Legacy Blueprint

This week, create a "Legacy Blueprint" for your life and business. Include:

- A list of core values you want to pass on.
- A vision statement for your legacy.

- Key individuals to mentor and invest in.
- Structures or systems that need to be built or documented.
- A list of unfinished dreams God may want others to complete through you.

Pray over this blueprint and take one step—however small—toward solidifying your legacy.

Consider writing a letter to your future successors. Share your heart, your prayers, and your dreams for what comes next. Let them hear your voice, not just see your results.

Final Thoughts

Legacy is not just what you leave behind—it's what you leave within others. It's the echo of your obedience. It's the fruit of faithfulness planted in secret and harvested in future generations.

Like David, you may not build everything you dream. But you can prepare the next generation to build even more.

The greatest leaders aren't those who finish first. They're the ones who leave the baton in the hands of those who finish well.

Let your life not just be successful—let it be significant.

Closing Prayer

Father, thank You for the privilege of building something that lasts. Help me to lead with legacy in mind. Let my life echo with eternal value. Teach me to prioritize people over platforms, impact over image, and faithfulness over fame.

Help me to sow seeds of wisdom, generosity, and integrity that will bless generations I may never meet. Let my business, my leadership, and my daily decisions point others to You.

May the generations that follow me walk in blessings I prayed for, live out promises I believed for, and fulfill purposes You planted through me.

In Jesus' name, Amen.

Conclusion

Obey and Build

If there's one truth that echoes through every page of this book, it's this:

Your obedience matters.

In the world's eyes, your yes to God may look small—like a whisper, a delay, a pivot, a no one else understands. But in Heaven's economy, that yes can shake nations, shift generations, and unlock eternal outcomes.

You don't need to be the loudest voice or the biggest name.

You just need to be faithful.

Obey in the boardroom.

Obey in the quiet of your morning prayer.

Obey when it costs you something.

Obey when it seems insignificant.

Every step of obedience is a seed. And when God breathes on it, the impact multiplies far beyond what you could ever ask or imagine.

As you close this book, don't rush to the next project.

Pause. Reflect. Ask God,

"What's the next small step You're asking me to take?"

Then take it.

Your legacy won't be built in a single moment.

It will be forged over time—through a lifestyle of obedient surrender.

Let's build with God, not just for Him.

Let's obey now… and trust Him with the outcome.

Acknowledgments

I want to begin by thanking Jesus Christ—my Lord, my redeemer, and my God. Without the clear sound of His voice, this book would not be possible. Every revelation, every chapter, and every moment of clarity was birthed through obedience to Him.

To my wife, Roselly—thank you for your unwavering love, strength, and spiritual depth. Your obedience, encouragement, and belief in me were the foundation upon which this book was built. You are my greatest blessing.

To our daughters—you are my daily inspiration. I pray this book helps shape a world in which you seek obedience to Christ as your greatest strength.

To my family and friends—thank you for your constant prayers, patience, and love throughout this process.

To my Faith & Business brothers and sisters—thank you for walking this journey with me. Your accountability, insight, and encouragement sharpened me and pushed this message forward.

To our team and backers at The Center for Faith & Business—thank you for believing in this vision and helping bring it to life. This book is just one step in what we are building together for God's Kingdom.

To every person who ever sowed a word of encouragement, a prayer, a connection, or a simple "keep going"—thank you. Your impact is greater than you know.

Finally, to the readers of this book—thank you for opening your heart to what God is doing in the marketplace. May your yes to Him shape the world in ways we've yet to imagine.

About the Author

Darrel Frater is a Kingdom-driven entrepreneur, investor, and author committed to helping leaders build businesses rooted in faith, purpose, and lasting impact. With a professional background in venture capital and startup ecosystems, he has spent years supporting underestimated entrepreneurs and working to close wealth gaps through strategic investment and community-building.

His passion for faith and business is grounded in a deep conviction that entrepreneurship is more than an economic engine. It is a vehicle for transformation and a platform for advancing the Kingdom of God. Through his work, Darrel has helped elevate diverse founders, steward capital with integrity, and challenge systems that perpetuate inequality.

Darrel is the co-founder of The Center for Faith & Business, a 501c3 nonprofit organization that equips leaders to integrate biblical principles into their ventures, decision-making, and legacy.

He is also the Founder and Managing Partner of TGN Ventures, "The Good News," an early-stage investment firm backing funds and companies that expand economic mobility while pursuing strong, risk-adjusted returns.

Darrel lives in Tulsa, Oklahoma with his wife, Roselly, and their daughters, Gianna and Moriah. Together they are building family, legacy, and faith, one act of obedience at a time.

To connect with Darrel or learn more, visit www.DarrelFrater.com.

Resources & Next Steps

Thank you for taking this journey.

My prayer is that this book did more than inspire you. I pray it activates something within you to walk in radical obedience and build with God in every area of your life.

If you are ready to take the next step, here are ways to stay connected and continue growing:

---

1. **The Center for Faith & Business**
   Join a growing movement of Kingdom-minded leaders integrating faith and business to influence culture, shift systems, and build legacy.

   Learn more:
   https://BuildWithFaith.org

---

2. **The Good News Founder Community**
   Join our free founder community and walk alongside other builders who are committed to stewarding their assignments with excellence and eternal impact.

   Join here:
   https://bit.ly/TGNFoundersCommunity

---

3. **Devotionals, Workbooks, and Digital Tools**
   Access supplemental resources designed to help you go deeper:

   - Guided devotionals for faith-driven entrepreneurs
   - Business vision and Kingdom strategy templates
   - Recorded teachings and online workshops

   Explore resources:
   https://BuildWithFaith.org

---

4. **Speaking & Consulting**
   Interested in bringing this message to your church, company, or conference?

   Darrel is available for keynote speaking, leadership workshops, and business consulting grounded in biblical principles and practical execution.

   Inquire at: DarrelDFrater@gmail.com

---

5. **Investments**
   Partner with value-aligned investors committed to expanding God's Kingdom while pursuing strong, risk-adjusted returns.

   Learn more:
   https://TGNVentures.vc

---

6. **Share the Movement**
   If this book impacted you, help multiply the message:

   - Leave a review on Amazon or Goodreads
   - Gift a copy to a friend or colleague
   - Start a small group around the content
   - Tag @DarrelFrater and use #BuildWithFaith on social media

---

Obedience is not the end of your journey. It is the beginning.

Let's keep building together.

Scripture Index

Ephesians

Colossians

Micro Obedience, Macro Impact is my first book.

In the spirit of firstfruits, all proceeds from this book support the ongoing work of The Center for Faith & Business.

Join us in advancing the Gospel through business at: https://bit.ly/CFBGive

www.ingramcontent.com/pod-product-compliance
Ingram Content Group UK Ltd.
Pitfield, Milton Keynes, MK11 3LW, UK
UKHW041824200726
13854UKWH00002BA/538